The War We Never Fought

The British Establishment's Surrender to Drugs

Peter Hitchens

BLOOMSBURY
LONDON · BERLIN · NEW YORK · SYDNEY

First published in Great Britain 2012

© Peter Hitchens, 2012

The moral right of the author has been asserted

No part of this book may be used or reproduced in any manner whatsoever without written permission from the Publisher except in the case of brief quotations embodied in critical articles or reviews. Every reasonable effort has been made to trace copyright holders of material reproduced in this book, but if any have been inadvertently overlooked the Publishers would be glad to hear from them.

Bloomsbury Publishing Plc
50 Bedford Square
London WC1B 3DP

www.bloomsbury.com

Bloomsbury Publishing, London, Berlin, New York and Sydney

A CIP record for this book is available from the British Library.

ISBN: HB: 978-1-4411-7331-7

10 9 8 7 6 5 4 3 2 1

Typeset by Fakenham Prepress Solutions, Fakenham, Norfolk NR21 8NN
Printed and bound in Great Britain by CPI Group (UK) Ltd, Croydon, CR0 4YY

Contents

Acknowledgments vii
Preface xi

Part One The Secret Capitulation 1

1 Cannabis is a cause 3

2 How to sink, giggling, into the sea 13

3 Psychiatry is not an exact science 21

4 The real purpose of classification – a better image for cannabis 29

5 No use appealing to God. Try John Stuart Mill? 39

6 Cannabis and violence 47

7 What about alcohol and tobacco, then? 53

8 The Cabinet gets it wrong 61

9 Enter Richard Crossman 69

10 Jim Callaghan's last stand 77

Part Two The Search for Soma 83

11 Aldous Huxley 85

12 The left casts off its puritan garments 93

13 The mysterious spread of cannabis 99

14 Jaggerism is invented 111

15 Bloomsbury takes over Britain via the airwaves 119

16 Steve Abrams steps up to explain 129

17 The long march – Wootton and after 141

18 Widdecombe unfair 167

19 Dame Ruth Runciman and the liberal establishment 175

20 Legislation on the beat – Brian Paddick 199

21 The great red herring – 'medical marijuana' 225

22 Freeing up or freeing down? 233

23 Some notes on harm reduction and rehabilitation 243

24 The demoralisation of Britain 251

Index 269

Acknowledgments

Many people made me want to write this book, but they will not be very pleased to be given the credit for doing so. They are the legion of politicians, commentators, celebrities, ex-policemen, serving policemen, judges, lawyers and cultural figures who repeatedly insist that this country groans under the heel of an oppressive prohibition regime.

All of them ought to know better, and this book will enable them to know better. We shall then find out if their urgently-expressed opinions are based upon fact, or on some other foundation.

I owe a different sort of debt to Robin Baird-Smith, a superlative publisher who endures much when he has to, encourages when encouragement is needed, and listens when it matters most; to Peter Wright, Editor of the *Mail on Sunday* for most of the period during which I researched and wrote this book, who gave me freedom to pursue this subject, and provided essential support when it was not fashionable to do so, and most of the rest of Fleet Street was running the other way; To Kathy Gyngell of the Centre for Policy Studies, a valuable ally in the struggle against the liberalisers; to Mary Brett, whose unrelenting desire to protect the young from drugs with facts and logic deserves wider recognition; to the librarians at Associated Newspapers, friendly and helpful keepers of one of the most precious archives in the English language; to my elder son Daniel, who has now twice come to my rescue at a decisive moment in the making of a book, and to Nicola Rusk, who also played a major part in herding my prolix paragraphs into a coherent shape.

Above all, my thanks are due to my wife, Eve, from whom I must steal so much valuable time each time I set out to write a book, who must listen to my complaints and vows that I shall never again write a book (always broken) and who has to endure the reverses and difficulties without having the pleasures of scribbling.

They should share any credit. I take all the blame

For Eve

Preface

On a secret site somewhere in Southern England, as you read these words, a major drug company is quite legally growing large quantities of cannabis. The essential ingredients of the plant, packaged as a mouth-spray, are available on prescription from the National Health Service. It is said, though the evidence is open to contention, to alleviate some of the symptoms of multiple sclerosis. Perhaps, in time, it will have other applications.

On another not-so-secret site, near where the Chiltern Hills run gently down towards the Thames Valley at the Goring Gap, the observant traveller may in most summers see large fields of regimented opium poppies blooming (in some years the fields are left fallow). These, too, are grown, harvested and processed under licences issued by Her Majesty's Government. If they were not, the nearby Royal Air Force base at Benson might be required to destroy them from the sky. In this case the exotic and colourful harvest is used to produce medical morphine, ever more in demand for the sick and dying, who have benefited, or otherwise, from the ability of medical science to keep us alive against all odds, and the increasing desire of us all that the old should die out of sight, in vast remote hospitals.

Drugs and their relation to the law are a complicated subject. A crop that would bring down napalm upon an Afghan farmer is officially encouraged in Oxfordshire. Another crop, which the police would raid if it were in the loft of a suburban house, is providing officially sanctioned comfort to sufferers from a much-feared disease.

There is more. Each year, astonishing numbers of prescriptions are issued for drugs officially described as 'antidepressants'. Many of these are given to men and women living in areas where unemployment is high, or suffering other social ills.

Perhaps most surprising of all to an alien visiting from the recent past (and who or what could be more alien than such a person?) is the increasing prescription, to children in Britain and the USA, of such drugs as Adderall and Ritalin – one an amphetamine and the other with characteristics very similar to the amphetamines. These pills are supposed to improve the behaviour of children supposedly suffering from an ailment with no objectively measurable symptoms, called 'Attention Deficit Hyperactivity Disorder' ('ADHD'). They are also used to 'treat' children who are said to be in the throes of 'Oppositional Defiant Disorder' (ODD). I am not making this up.

Well, I have suffered, or in my view benefited, from 'Oppositional Defiant Disorder' since I emerged screaming into the world, 60 years ago, surrounded by anxiously praying Maltese nuns. And I am haunted and dismayed by the idea that, had I been born into the present age, it would have occurred to more than one of the adult institutions in which I was Oppositional and Defiant to turn me into a conformist by classifying my discontents as a 'Disorder' and prescribing me a little pill. This idea either nauseates you, or it does not. If it does not, then what follows is probably of little use to you.

Now, leaving all other considerations on this subject aside, I think it is important for our society to wonder why it has lately become so ready to accept that human woe can be cured or soothed by chemicals. These chemicals do not alter or reform the ills of our civilisation. They adapt the human being to them.

Later in this book you will find some interesting remarks made by Aldous Huxley, about the Brave New World of willing, even enthusiastic self-stupefaction which he feared we were embracing.

Having lived through the great moral, political and cultural convulsion that transformed my country and others between 1968 and today, I am struck by one great paradox. Most of us, as we cheered on the French students in Paris, or marched righteously against the Vietnam War, or expressed our scorn for the racial bigotry of our elders, or sought the end of puritan sexual rules, were united by one good bond. We loved liberty and hated tyranny. We were often, but not always, wrong about the causes we joined. But we were never apologists for serfdom and dull-witted, thoughtless contentment. If the world was awry, then we thought we should change it, not adapt ourselves to injustice and wrong.

Now, mysteriously, the 1968 generation have for the most part become supporters of drug 'decriminalisation', a cause whose success will inevitably mean more doped contentment and more willing serfdom. And in many cases they seek to equate the freedom to take stupefying drugs with its opposites, the freedoms of speech, thought and assembly.

As in so many other matters, the honourable and kindly instincts of the Left have produced – or are soon likely to produce – outcomes that no honourable or kind person could possibly desire. In almost everything that I have said or written I have tried to make this same point – that the Left cannot have foreseen or wanted the things they have brought about. Yet, again and again, rather than re-examine their principles and change their opinions, they have sought to blame others for the evils they have caused.

On this issue of drugs, they are now doing it again, ludicrously attributing the effects of 40 years of decriminalisation to a phantasmal 'War on Drugs' that has never been fought. I can only hope that this book manages to open a few generous minds to the truth, while preparing myself for the usual abuse.

Oxford, June 2012

Part One

The Secret Capitulation

Again and again I have had the satisfaction of seeing the laughable idealism of one generation evolve into the accepted commonplace of the next.
BARBARA WOOTTON, *IN A WORLD I NEVER MADE*, 1967

As political and economic freedom diminishes, sexual freedom tends compensatingly to increase. And the dictator (unless he needs cannon fodder and families with which to colonize empty or conquered territories) will do well to encourage that freedom. In conjunction with the freedom to daydream under the influence of dope and movies and the radio, it will help to reconcile his subjects to the servitude which is their fate.
ALDOUS HUXLEY, FOREWORD TO THE 1946 EDITION OF *BRAVE NEW WORLD*

1
Cannabis is a cause

Cannabis is not merely a drug. It is a cause. The social and cultural revolutionaries who have shaped modern Britain see the freedom to fuddle their own brains with chemical fumes as a pillar of human liberty.

For them, unfettered indulgence in a chemical stupor – which they like to call a right – is a matter of principle. It is comparable to the freedoms of speech and thought. They are sure that the law should not get in the way of it. They are puzzled by the suggestion that there may be a moral case against it. They view those who do not share this view as repressive tyrants.

The unholy and undivided trinity of 'Sex, Drugs and Rock and Roll' is not merely a slogan. This trio of self-indulgences is the tripod on which modern morality rests. All three exalt the self. All three involve sensual pleasure sought for its own sake, separated from any effort or responsibility. Drug taking is the purest form of self-indulgence. It is permitted and promoted by the new morality, because it is the perfect, sublime version of the pursuit of present pleasure.

They do not care that it smothers thought and dilutes discontent, the very things that real lovers of human liberty need and value. This is because the search for present pleasure has replaced an older purpose – the pursuit of future happiness, either earthly or heavenly, often through self-denial and sacrifice. Of course the movement for weaker drug laws does not like to put it like that. So it clothes itself in the shining robes of liberty, and dismisses the older view, mistrustful of instant gratification, as repressed, narrow and cruel.

Drug taking, which separates reward from effort, walks in step with the sexual revolution, which separates the sex act from fertility, and so also separates it from marriage, patience, fidelity and constancy. It also marches in time with the successful campaign to end the taboo against pornography, ludicrously disguised as a battle against censorship.

Drug taking is allied, above all, with modern popular music. This music preaches the gospel of self. Its self-pitying, self-indulgent and self-righteous lyrics are frequently crammed with drug references, explicit or coded, and the musicians themselves, who are admired as idols and examples, are often enthusiastic drug-takers. It also selfishly stimulates the senses, particularly the sexual urge and the urge to violence and greed, with blasts of pure fierce volume. It has followed quickly after the dismantling of religion and adult authority. The allied forces of parental power and Christian morals were until recently able to make the young postpone pleasure and defer gratification. Now these influences are almost gone, there is no reason to wait.

The belief in instant gratification also helps the demolition of the literary and musical canons. There is no longer an accepted body of knowledge which needs to be learned. Criticism, sometimes for its own sake, is more important than the original text and teachers have no authority but are mere facilitators.

As a result, there is no longer any objective measure of learning in the arts. Examinations can be passed without actually reading the original texts under discussion. Modern writing is given equal status to the classics. Wide historical knowledge is disregarded in favour of empathy or confusing 'sources' which encourage the idea that there is no objective truth to be found about the past. Even graduates of Oxford University are obtaining degrees despite being unable to spell and being unfamiliar with important areas of what would once have been indispensable, essential knowledge. Many, for instance, have no idea who Mr Micawber was.[1] Historical knowledge among the graduate young is also full of vast gaps and misunderstandings.

The young are encouraged to think themselves educated when they are not, often by teachers who are themselves uneducated. Education is said to be 'child-centred'. In all things, the liberated, unrestrained sovereign self is in charge. How, in such a world, could drug taking be wrong?

Our current economic crisis, which seems likely to be permanent, is largely caused by another aspect of this festival of self-gratification. The astonishing transformation of individual and official attitudes towards debt has led millions of people to spend huge sums of money they have not got and never will have. Debt is now seen as normal rather than shameful, and thrift is viewed as pointless and even foolish. Governments, too, have become far more indebted than they would ever have dared to be before.

Mind-altering drugs have from the beginning been an important feature of this new post-Christian way of life. They have helped to bring it about. They are at the heart of the new belief in undeferred gratification. They were the shared pleasure, the unholy communion and the initiation rite, of the post-1968 cultural and moral revolutionaries. Those who accept that way of life can seldom see any reason why drug taking might be wrong or even unwise. It is part of the power of drugs that they make it easier to enjoy cultural mediocrity and to

---

[1] Oxford University examiners' reports, quoted in *The Daily Telegraph*, 23 January 2012.

endure decline of all kinds – moral, educational, cultural, political and material. A generation which began by thinking itself revolutionary has adopted drugs which spread passivity and contentment.

Yet there is an important difference between drugs and the other features of the moral and cultural revolution. Millions of people, browbeaten into accepting the rest of the post-modern package, still find drugs disgusting and frightening. Many fear that their children will damage themselves by becoming drug users. This danger is widely viewed as an unpredictable and accidental fate quite beyond the control of adults. In some respects, this is true, since parents and responsible teachers have very little influence set beside the huge power of a culture which views drug taking as inevitable and not especially bad, and whose leading figures ceaselessly urge decriminalisation of drugs.

Yet despite decades of propaganda for decriminalisation and 'harm reduction' policies, many voters refuse to accept that the legalisation of cannabis is a wise or good aim. They are supported by several international treaties, which still bind the British government to maintain laws against certain named drugs.

That is why the legalisation of drugs in this country has been pursued so dishonestly, and so stealthily. Other deep changes in our civilisation, in attitudes towards marriage, parenthood, crime and personal responsibility, have been achieved more or less openly. But the *de facto* decriminalisation of drugs in this country has been so effectively camouflaged that most people do not yet realise that it has taken place. The thing has happened, but those responsible will not publicly admit that it has. Worse, those who wish it to go further, towards complete *de jure* legalisation, pretend that drug users still face serious legal repression.

This pretence has been so successful that many people still seriously believe that the criminal justice system is harsh towards individual drug users. Worse, many well-regarded commentators believe in this fictional persecution. They then blame it for several common social ills of our age.

We have been in this twilight zone for decades. The issues raised were well-described as long ago as 1972[2] by the author and broadcaster Malcolm Muggeridge, who had lived in Egypt during the 1920s when cannabis was widely and openly used there. Remarking that drug legalisation's supporters were nowadays 'respected citizens, clergymen, purported scientific investigators and other ostensibly informed and enlightened persons', he wrote:

> When I hear or read their apologies for hashish, I recall the Zaffaran Palace[3] and the stupefied faces and inert minds of so many of the students there; the dreadful instances of the destructive effect of this drug on bodies and minds which any resident in the Middle East was bound to encounter. I know of no better exemplification of the death wish at the heart of our way of life than this determination to bring about the legalisation of hashish so that it may ravage the West as it has the Middle and Far East.

In my book *A Brief History of Crime*,[4] I coupled Muggeridge's exasperated jeers with words from Allan Bloom's cry of despair at the slow death of proper education, *The Closing of the American Mind*. Bloom, as a teacher, had met many students who took drugs. He coupled rock music with those drugs, saying both provided 'premature ecstasy' and formed a close alliance in western youth culture. But he also hit upon the severe truth that this ecstasy is not just premature, but unearned. He argued that it breaks the link

---

[2] In his autobiography *Chronicles of Wasted Time*.
[3] Then the seat of Cairo University.
[4] Atlantic Books, 2003.

between effort, achievement and joy. He did not say – he was not a conservative – that by doing so it fatally injured the link between hard work and deferred reward which has been so important in the great Protestant Christian civilisations. But the implication is quite clear.

He was surely right to connect rock music and drugs. The two swagger across the devastated cultural landscape of our time, side by side and hand in fist. Rock music heroes and heroines are with few exceptions known for their unashamed drug taking. Many have died from it, drowned in vomit. Rock music – especially when allied with the enormously powerful sound systems of today, capable of shaking buildings – is close to being a drug itself. It is sometimes a stimulant and sometimes a depressant, but always influential over the moods of its listeners, often driven home by several megatons of noise. Its drug-laced lyrics are the hymns, psalms and anthems of the religion of self that became the dominant faith of Western humanity during the twentieth century.

Drugs and rock music, Bloom points out, have similar effects. Both artificially produce the 'exaltation naturally attached to the completion of the greatest endeavours – victory in a just war, consummated love, artistic creation, religious devotion and discovery of the truth'. Now that exaltation can be gained by 'anyone and everyone', Bloom goes on, 'without effort, without talent, without virtue, without the exercise of the faculties'.

Professor Bloom explains the great attraction of drugs and rock music to so many. He also demonstrates just why they have become so important in the decline of the great Western Christian nations. They democratise our culture, removing the need for deep reading or understanding, or for the long nurture of talent through learning. They offer its rewards and pleasures to all. They seem to supersede the tiresome Protestant ethic. They make deferred gratification appear a waste of time and a foolish rejection of readily available delight.

In this, they are very similar to the football superstars, lottery winners and wealthy celebrities who persuade so many young people that a pleasant life is available without study or training. This is sad, but not shocking among the uneducated and ignorant. It is far worse to find that the layers of society which ought to be defending high culture, effort, self-discipline and patience are just as morally corrupt as the young men and women who brawl and spew in the midnight streets of our great cities. And, as always, the corruption of the best is the worst of all.

Like all promises of unearned joy, these drugs present their accounts later, often too late ever to be paid in full. Bloom rather heartbreakingly recounts:

> In my experience, students who have had a serious fling with drugs – and gotten over it – find it difficult to have enthusiasms or great expectations. It is as though the colour has been drained out of their lives and they see everything in black and white. The pleasure they experienced in the beginning was so intense that they no longer look for it at the end or as the end. They may function perfectly well, but dryly, routinely. Their energy has been sapped, and they do not expect their life's activity to do anything but produce a living.

In a harsh metaphor: he ends by saying that as long as they have music pumping into their ears 'they cannot hear what the great tradition has to say. And after its prolonged use, when they take it off, they find they are deaf'.

Nobody ever meant it to be this bad. Neither Richard Crossman nor Tony Crosland nor Roy Jenkins – the politicians who did so much to create Britain's new society – intended this outcome. As we will see, these reformers thought they could limit the effects, as they licensed a more liberated society. They wanted a set of eclectic reforms. Their books speak of such things as longer alcohol licensing hours, brighter streetlamps, morality-free sex, the treatment of crime as a disease rather than the punishment of crime as an evil, continental cafes, and greater gaiety, all mixed up together. If they had an ideology or a dogma, they did not know it. They mainly knew what they were against, the plain, workful world of Anglo-Saxon Protestantism.

They do not seem to have thought that abandoning so many restraints at once might be risky. They do not seem to have considered that these annoying rules might have been there for a good reason. They truthfully pointed out that the old way of life was often grim. They then mistakenly concluded that it must therefore be wholly swept away.

Their decision to include drugs – and particularly cannabis – in their list of freedoms seems to have concerned them more than their other reforms. They did not have serious misgivings about what they did. But they realised that such a change would be widely unpopular and viewed as irresponsible by many. Still, they were convinced that they knew better, and so chose to pursue it. But with some cunning, they pretended to continue serious efforts to restrain the use of illegal drugs in our society. Indeed, the Cabinet's incoherent, illogical deliberations in February 1970 suggest that they were also trying to conceal this cunning from themselves. It is hard to explain the contradictory gibberish of post-1970 British drugs policy in any other way. The campaigners for decriminalisation, as we shall see, knew exactly what they were doing. The politicians who listened to them preferred to conceal the truth from themselves.

The resulting mess – Britain's nonsensical, ineffectual and illogical drug law – has for long been a scandal in its own right. Its contradictions and ambiguities are – as this author agrees – absurd. But they are not absurd for the reasons advanced by those who now argue for yet more relaxation. These activists assert that the law itself causes crime. This is, in a way, true of all laws and of all crimes. They also say that a campaign of stern prohibition has failed, and so must be abandoned.

But it has not failed. It could not have failed, because it has not been tried. It cannot be abandoned because it does not exist.

Advocates of decriminalisation have pretended – for propaganda purposes – that the existing state of affairs is cruel, repressive and draconian.

This falsehood needs to be shown for what it is. But anyone seriously interested in social policy should also take this chance to examine the general state of the drug laws in this country. Calls for their reform – in fact for their liberalisation to the point where they vanish – are frequent and are supported by many influential men and women. They are likely to succeed.

Almost certainly, the battle to halt the spread of mind-altering drugs is lost. The general decriminalisation of drugs will almost certainly happen in the next ten years or so. This change will help this country down the staircase which leads to Third World conditions of life, a staircase down which we are enthusiastically skipping in so many ways, educational, cultural, moral and legal, while somehow expecting that at the end of it life will remain as civilised as it was before.

Drug decriminalisation, by its very nature, will make it harder to sustain a competent, thoughtful, self-disciplined, hard-working and efficient society. It will also create contentment and apathy where discontent and a passion for reform should be.

2

How to sink, giggling, into the sea

But before we as a country sink giggling into the sea, we might at least consider things as they really are, and not as the pro-drug propagandists would like us to think they are. If we are to join the Third World – and some may find the idea more attractive than they are ready to admit – let us at least do so knowingly and wilfully, and not because we were fooled into it.

To begin with, we must understand just how long ago a morally relaxed governing class gave up the struggle on this important issue.

The British establishment formally surrendered to the drugs culture at a Cabinet meeting shortly before lunch on Thursday 26 February 1970. It was the quiet end of a war that had been surprisingly brief and gentle, if not actually phoney. Since that date there has been no serious official resistance to the view that the *use* of drugs, especially cannabis, is inevitable and not especially damaging. It is generally accepted that those who use them are either the pitiable victims of others or are pursuing a reasonable pleasure that is no business of the state.

At the same time there has been a frenzied official hostility to the production and sale of the same drugs. But this hostility is made almost entirely futile by the law's leniency towards the purchasers of the very substance whose supply and sale is considered so villainous.

This contradictory, self-defeating hysteria has successfully given the impression – to incurious observers – that a non-existent 'War against Drugs' is taking place.

The public, who in most cases think that there should be such a war against drugs, are reassured by this fiction. They should not be. Those who want drugs such as cannabis to be entirely legal, and who know perfectly well that they have almost achieved their ends, benefit from this fiction. They enjoy claiming that the supposed 'War' is cruel and has failed, despite being savagely waged. They go on to allege that this phantasmal 'War' is the cause of many evils and crimes.

The idea is spread, in debate and in popular TV dramas such as *The Wire*, that most of the evils caused by drug abuse would end if we legalised drugs. This change, it is argued, would break the connection between drugs and criminal gangs. It would also enable drugs to be sold in 'safe' quantities and without 'impurities'. This argument claims that the law, not the drug, is the problem.

A moment's thought shows the weakness of this case. It is a propaganda point, not a reasoned argument. We make laws because we have good reasons to do so. If nothing were illegal, we would not have any of the often ugly and costly side effects of law enforcement – prosecutions, prisons, black markets in illegal goods, criminal gangs organised to circumvent the law. If we legalised burglary and the receipt of stolen goods, for instance, there would be a boom in the sale of those stolen goods. In many cases they would be sold back to those who had been robbed in the first place, as was common in eighteenth-century London. The police would have much less to do, and insurance companies might lose many premiums. To some extent this is already happening in the more lawless parts of modern Britain.

But most people who suffer burglary are distressed and angered. They wish that the law against it was more fiercely enforced so that it would not happen to them. The logic of 'less law, less crime' forgets that crime has unpleasant effects on its victims: the very reason why laws came into being in the first place. We accept all the disadvantages and costs of law enforcement, because properly enforced laws deter various kinds of behaviour that make our society less civilised. In short, the 'less law, less crime' arguments avoid the real question, which is whether there is a good reason to make certain drugs illegal in the first place.

The drugs named in the Misuse of Drugs Act 1971 (and in its more potent forerunners, the Dangerous Drugs Acts) are illegal for a simple reason. The state still accepts that, even in their pure form, there is no safe dose. All drugs are regulated in some way by law, even undoubtedly beneficial ones such as antibiotics. They cannot be dispensed without a doctor's prescription. In Britain, even mild painkillers (such as the mixture of paracetamol with small amounts of codeine) cannot be sold directly from the shelves.

This process of licensing and regulation is actually far more complex than it first appears. It is crammed with moral difficulties. By licensing a drug for medical use, the state provides a seal of scientific approval, based on the drug's effectiveness in treating illness, balanced against its risks and side effects. Sometimes, it miscalculates badly, as in the case of thalidomide, prescribed as a cure for morning sickness but leading to terrible deformities among babies. Its current readiness to see the widespread prescription of SSRI (Selective Serotonin Re-uptake Inhibitors) 'anti-depressants' seems likely to lead to severe controversy before too long, as doubts are cast on their efficacy and as worries grow about their possible unwanted side effects.

By licensing a drug for recreational use, the state provides a seal of moral approval, based on a complicated and shifting calculus of pleasure set against social and medical damage. Chemists in Britain do not sell cigarettes or gin. But they do sell Viagra and 'morning-after pills', the one to enhance pleasure, the other to ensure that pleasure does not bring undesired (but perfectly natural) consequences. Both these preparations would have disturbed the morals of 30 years ago, and outraged those of 60 years ago. The licensing decision is not merely technical. Were they to allow chemists (or anyone else) to sell cannabis preparations, they would be saying that this drug's risks and disadvantages were counterbalanced by its pleasures. They would also be saying that a particular kind of pleasure, that of being intoxicated, was officially approved of.

All drugs are themselves dangerous by their very nature, especially in the hands of people who know little about them. That is why the law is designed to restrict their use. Take some more examples. Leaving aside its possible but unmeasured effects on mental health, cocaine, especially in its smoked form, has serious effects on the heart. In powder form it can physically destroy the user's nose. It is also associated with strokes, brain haemorrhages, hypothermia, agitated delirium, cardiac arrest, irregular heart rhythm and convulsions. It may make people behave more badly than they would if they had not taken it. In an analysis of 1,000 people arrested for violent offences in Greater Manchester, more than 400 tested positive for cocaine use.

Heroin is likewise extremely bad for the user's metabolism, general health and longevity, most especially if needles are shared with other users, as they often are. This, as is now well known, can lead to severe infections being transferred from user to user. Large-scale habitual users of all these drugs often (though not always) make themselves unfit for productive work. They become at one and the same time devoted to an expensive pleasure and unable to work to pay for it because they are either too stupefied or too agitated by the desire for more. This is why they so often take to ruthless thieving, often from their own close family, and increasingly from the taxpayer, who provides them with methadone, a substitute pleasure. This combination of costly indulgence and disinclination to work is surely one we should not encourage. But how else, apart from laws forbidding and punishing its possession, are we to discourage it effectively? Indulgence and so-called 'treatment' have certainly not done so.

Some users of heroin are or become the parents of children, whose living conditions and hopes of a happy life thereafter are frequently appalling. Once again, it is hard to see how this can be prevented or discouraged, except by strongly enforced laws against the possession of the drug itself.

Those who oppose such laws often argue that the indulgence of heroin users is the solution. Their arguments, widely praised by media commentators and 'advanced' politicians, have had a powerful effect on national policy in several countries, including our own. But these measures simply transfer the crime from the individual to the state. Rather than compel the criminal drug user to abandon his habit, the authorities force bus-drivers, postmen, doctors, nurses and school dinner-ladies to buy stupefying drugs for criminal parasites, who would otherwise steal directly to obtain them. The phrase 'legalised theft' can seldom have been more apt.

How is this done? In many cases the users (often including convicted prisoners in custody) can nowadays persuade the state to provide them with methadone or other substitutes for heroin. The annual national bill for supplying drug-takers with methadone is roughly £300 million, not much less than the £380 million spent on trying to control the supply of illegal drugs. Criminal drug abusers are mollified by the taxpayer-funded prescription of a legal substitute. This sordid and cowardly arrangement goes by the misleading name of 'treatment'.

In many of these cases the recipients then illegally sell the methadone to buy heroin, which they prefer. Frightening numbers of such people become permanent burdens on the taxpayer until they die. Under current non-punitive policies, they face no serious pressure to abandon their habit, let alone pay for their own keep.

Much of this activity relies on general acceptance of the dubious concept of 'addiction', an essentially circular and unscientific term which is accepted without discussion by modern societies. Theodore Dalrymple, in his book *Romancing Opiates*, has rightly cast doubt on the myth of near-insuperable physical addiction, as absurdly portrayed in the film *French Connection 2*. Since Dr Dalrymple was for many years a prison physician, with direct experience of many drug abusers, his doubts must be taken seriously. The effect of the word, Dalrymple argues, is to take responsibility away from the individual involved, and to transform him from a wilful criminal (in the case of illegal drugs such as heroin), and a greedy person with poor self-control, into a pitiable victim of an uncontrollable force. Thanks to this transformation, he requires help, hospitals and subsidies rather than punishment and prison.

It is astonishing that what is in fact a moral revolution – in which free will has been abolished – has been presented to the public over the past half-century as some sort of scientific fact. Many drugs are habit-forming (tobacco probably most of all) but it is false to suggest that those who use them cannot, if they wish, cease to do so. It is difficult but it is not in any way physically impossible. The complaint known as 'addiction', like so many other pseudo-medical conditions nowadays recognised by doctors, cannot be objectively diagnosed or detected by recognised physical or chemical tests. It is also important to note that all successful 'anti-addiction' programmes invariably rely on one common ingredient, the supposed addict's genuine desire to cease being an addict. Mysteriously, if he does not want to stop, he will not do so. This has been found again and again by Alcoholics Anonymous.

The dangers of cannabis are less well-documented, partly because it is extremely difficult to run trials of a drug which may or not cause permanent irreversible mental illness. It cannot be tested on animals. That would be hideous as well as useless. Should it be tested on humans, knowing what we know and suspecting what we suspect? This question is more urgent than most suspect. There is, in a sense, such a test now under way, since the licensing in Britain for medical use of a drug based on the ingredients of cannabis. It is to be hoped that its use is monitored carefully and systematically.

We can at least say, thanks to a large number of studies of admitted cannabis users, that there appears to be a correlation between cannabis use and some form of mental illness, necessarily loosely defined. It can also be said that many people are aware of such a correlation in the lives of individuals known to them, anecdotal evidence so common that it would be unwise to ignore it.

One such anecdote is the dismal story of Henry Cockburn. It is told by Henry himself, and by his father, the distinguished foreign correspondent Patrick Cockburn, in their painfully frank 2011 book *Henry's Demons*. Henry seems to have begun smoking cannabis as a bright and healthy schoolboy aged around 12. By his late teens, he was having severe and disturbing episodes of irrational and delusional behaviour, which ended with his being placed in the locked ward of a mental hospital and dosed with powerful antipsychotic medication. He is still taking antipsychotic medication and there is no indication that he will ever be able to cease doing so. It has, as do all such treatments, grave side effects. Henry's life has been radically altered for the worse, and it is at least possible that his use of cannabis is one of the main causes of this. Many parents of the current generation of teenagers are aware of similar cases where hard fact is lacking but suspicion is strong. Yet somehow they have yet to coalesce into the sort of evidence on which governments will act. How should we view this information?

The Cockburns' harrowing account strongly correlates youthful cannabis smoking with later mental illness. That should be no surprise. Such a correlation has long been noticed by many people in close touch with young men and women, such as parents, doctors and teachers, and has been growing more striking as the use of cannabis increases.

But it is hard to resolve it into causation, for several reasons. The categories of 'mental illness' are not objectively measurable or consistent. Such diagnoses as 'psychosis' or 'schizophrenia' vary greatly and are largely subjective. They are not like lung cancer, heart disease or emphysema, measurable physical complaints with objective symptoms. Neurology, the actual objective study, diagnosis and treatment of physically measurable disorders of the brain, is in its infancy. It is limited by the great delicacy of the brain, by its inaccessibility and by the difficulty of examining the brain tissues of a living person. Scans of various sorts may tell us a little. But we know a good deal less than most people suppose. In recent years, following the development of several mind-altering drugs, notably SSRI 'antidepressants', neurology has quietly given place to the new discipline of neuropsychopharmacology. This is a curious mixture of psychiatry, psychology, neurology and pharmacology which may be less than the sum of its parts. Some of these disciplines are exact and objectively measurable. Others are not. Its certainties on the treatment of depression have recently been challenged by distinguished doctors, including the American medical academic Dr Marcia Angell.

3
Psychiatry is not an exact science

Psychiatry makes large and bold claims for its knowledge and understanding of people's mental states. But while its practitioners are medically qualified (by contrast with psychologists, often mistaken by the public for psychiatrists), much of what they know, or say they know, is necessarily subjective and vague. The great Freudian theory on which much psychiatry was based is now doubted and disputed. Techniques such as pre-frontal lobotomy have now been discredited. Electro-convulsive therapy, still in use, is open to severe doubt.

The boundaries of psychiatric illness and disorders are vague and subject to change over time. The huge growth in cases of autism is one example of this, as is the epidemic of 'depression' which has accompanied the development of SSRI drugs which claim to treat it (a claim increasingly disputed by qualified doctors). A very large number of children are said to be suffering from contentious complaints such as 'Dyslexia' or 'ADHD' (Attention Deficit Hyperactivity Disorder), for which no objective physical or biochemical tests are available. This subjective diagnosis suits the interests of parents (absolved from responsibility for their children's misbehaviour), teachers (absolved from responsibility for their inability to maintain order and sustain interest in their classrooms) doctors (who can please patients and pharmaceutical companies by prescribing a drug), pharmaceutical companies (profiting from the widespread prescription of their drugs) and a whole industry of social workers and others whose employment relies on the recognition of this or that 'disorder' as a reality.

A similar vagueness, leaning in the other direction, quite possibly leads to the severe undercounting of the number of young people whose minds have been permanently altered by illegal drugs. Perhaps this will change if the pharmaceutical industry develops a drug which claims to treat the effects of cannabis.

Nothing is impossible in this vague area. The American Psychiatric Association, whose Diagnostic and Statistical Manual of Mental Disorders (DSM) is the generally accepted standard for mental health diagnoses, changes its views radically over time. At one time, for instance, it classified homosexuality as a disorder. Now it does not. This change is clearly the result of changing ethics and cultural norms, not the result of any change in homosexuality itself. This is an extreme example. The classifications of other mental disorders, which are awarded grandiose Greek names to make their descriptions appear rigorously scientific, also shift over time. Following a recent dispute about the nature of schizophrenia, diagnoses of this complaint fell sharply among psychiatrists who followed the DSM.

These blurred boundaries mean that many people live and work in advanced societies without ever being diagnosed as suffering from a mental illness, as long as they do not in some way trouble the authorities. Yet that does not mean they are undamaged by drugs which they have taken. A large welfare state, which houses and supports many marginal and chaotic unemployed people, allows them to continue to subsist more-or-less-adequately and has no great interest in classifying them as mentally ill. In fact, it often has a strong interest in not doing so, as expensive drugs might then be prescribed, or even more costly hospital beds.

These sufferers see no benefit to themselves in being listed as mentally ill – a diagnosis which might lead to detention or the forcible prescription of mind-altering drugs.

Even so, they may have suffered severe academic setbacks at a crucial moment in their teens. They may have lost ambition and self-discipline. They may have heard voices in their heads, developed mild persecution mania, experienced hallucinations. They may be unemployable and easy victims for thieves and bullies, but otherwise ignored by society. They may be among the growing and distressing class of people known misleadingly as 'homeless', but whose real lack is not just that of a roof, but of an ordered and productive life, a supportive family, a circle of friends, the real possibility of obtaining work.

Drug taking is common in this group. Is it unreasonable to suggest that in at least some cases the drug taking is among the causes of their condition? Yet how could this be definitively established? Defenders of drugs will always argue that such people take drugs to 'self-medicate' in response to their conditions. The idea is medically absurd, as no serious treatment is possible without precisely measured doses of a drug taken according to a doctor's instruction. Plainly, smoking or eating street cannabis cannot meet these criteria. Such 'self-medication' is suspected by some doctors of making these patients worse than they were before. But without extremely expensive and time-consuming research, which no established institution currently wishes to conduct, we cannot settle this for certain and may in fact never be able to. But do we need total certainty to act wisely?

Another interesting example of the way in which official fact gathering might miss cannabis users is provided in an unexpected place. It is to be found in a report often used by the pro-drug lobby to dismiss worries about cannabis and mental illness. This is the Keele University Study: 'Assessing the impact of cannabis use on trends in diagnosed schizophrenia in the United Kingdom from 1996 to 2005'. The survey concluded there was no evidence of a connection. But in doing so, it made heavy use of the General Practice Research Database. Normally, this would be a reliable way of measuring the prevalence of a problem. Roughly 95 per cent of the United Kingdom population is registered with a general medical practitioner.

Its figures on cannabis use among the mentally ill might seem to be satisfactory, if you accepted that the vague and shifting boundaries of mental illness can be consistently and reliably calibrated.[1]

But it is possible, and in fact probable, that it is misleading. Those most likely to be badly affected by cannabis use are also likely to be disproportionately concentrated among the unregistered 5 per cent. Those who fail to register with General Practitioners tend to be those on the fringes of society, unsettled, unemployed, chaotic, moving frequently, living in multi-occupation buildings in poor areas with inadequate GP services, or indeed homeless and living in doorways or under bridges. They are likely, if ill, to attend hospital casualty departments rather than General Practitioners. It is also the case that widespread cannabis use among sub-teenagers (12–15 years old) has only become a major problem recently. Since it seems likely that the risks of cannabis are greater for younger users, the Keele Study may simply have come too early to detect their problems.

Hospital statistics, it is true, also show a fall in schizophrenia and psychosis admissions. But the Keele report quite rightly concedes that 'the latter data could be due to policy, 'e.g. less care for such patients in hospital settings'. This is very likely, in the economising days of

---

[1] This is in fact a questionable view, as discussed above, p.21.

'Care in the Community' when the British health system is trying very hard to avoid putting the mentally ill in long-term hospital care. Doctors are well aware of this. So are potential mental patients. Such people might easily attend hospital casualty departments, already busy with drunken violence and traffic casualties, and be recorded only as being physically ill.

In any case, what do the words 'psychosis' and 'schizophrenia' really mean? They can mean severe hallucinations and total irrationality, even homicidal violence. They can also involve symptoms far less dramatic and obvious than these. If we judged them only slightly differently, might there be rather more sufferers?

But it is in the interests of many people to limit the diagnosis of mental illness in such a way that the damage done by cannabis is not officially recorded. Some simply want such diagnoses restricted to those with the most marked symptoms. The National Health Service, constantly short of money, seeks to treat the mentally ill 'in the community' rather than in cash-hungry hospitals. But such 'care in the community' is expensive too, because of the need for drugs and social workers. The British political and cultural establishment wishes for various reasons, discussed elsewhere in this book, to minimise the dangers of cannabis.

I accept that these facts do not provide a conclusive argument. Much experience of this debate convinces me that we will never find such an argument, as long as human knowledge of the functioning of the brain remains at its current levels, and as long as there is no huge political or commercial drive for research on the subject (which there most emphatically is not – the interest and the money are all on the other side). In a brief separate chapter, I will recount the experiences of those who warned for years about the dangers of tobacco. I hope only to illustrate here that the widespread complacency of the legalisation lobby, about the dangers of cannabis, is indefensible.

Those who do not wish to listen to the informed and cogent warnings of leading scientists will find excuses not to do so. They will ignore, for example, one of Britain's leading psychiatrists, Professor Sir Robin Murray of the Maudsley Hospital in London. Professor Murray has little doubt about the correlation between cannabis use and mental illness. He argues that teenagers, especially younger teenagers, are more vulnerable in this regard than adults, which could be another explanation for the failure of schizophrenia figures to reflect the growing level of use of cannabis in this country. Cannabis use among under-16s has only become significant very recently, and its effects may not show in statistics for some time. A significant pointer is cited in a longitudinal study of schizophrenia patients in South London.[2] This suggests that an explanation is necessary for the doubling of the incidence of schizophrenia in south-east London in the three decades since 1965.

As south-east London has been affected for longer, and more intensely, by the cultural and moral revolution in Britain than most other parts of the country, increased use of psychotropic drugs is a plausible explanation for some of this increase.

Sir Robin is not a lightweight figure, and he is by no means alone, though it is necessary to say that his view is not universally shared in his profession.

Another major longitudinal study of Swedish Army conscripts offers further suggestive indications of a link between cannabis and mental illness. I do not intend here to set out all the many research papers which deal with this subject and tend in the same direction. I do not think we can expect any total scientific certainty on this subject in my lifetime. But that does not absolve us from

---

[2] 'Incidence of schizophrenia in south-east London between 1965 and 1997', British Journal of Psychiatry 2008, Boydell and others, Vol. 182, pp.45–9.

responsibility. If there is no certainty, there is strong probability. Should we then do nothing?

It is, in any case, hardly far-fetched to suggest that a drug whose main effect is to alter the behaviour of the human brain might impair the working of that brain in at least some cases. Surely it is more fanciful to think that it would not do so.

The risk may be greatest among younger users. Its use among schoolchildren and students is also often very damaging to their work. Teachers in secondary schools frequently say that it can cause permanent and irrecoverable setbacks to their pupils' careers and futures. Research on the disadvantages of cannabis is for some reason not as commonly pursued as one might hope. But the 'anecdotal' complaint is frequent.

Many of these effects *are felt mainly by other people*. The cannabis user often has no idea that he has done himself any harm – a grave problem in debating this matter with people who support decriminalisation because they already use the drug and believe themselves to be unaffected. They will almost always insist that it has done them no damage. But they are in a poor position to know, as few people can observe themselves objectively. Also, none of us can know if we might have been more intelligent, more inventive and more energetic than we now are, if we had not irreversibly altered our brains by using drugs.

Since these drugs were made illegal, nothing has happened to suggest that they are safe. On the contrary, there are many indications that cannabis, in particular, may have dangers that were not suspected at the time of the 1971 Act. The principal active ingredient of cannabis, tetrahydrocannabinol, had only recently been discovered (1964) when the Wootton Committee (chaired by Baroness Wootton of Abinger, the veteran, left-wing, liberal battleaxe) was set up, and the report mentions it only in passing, while relying heavily on the ancient report into 'Indian Hemp'[3] and the New York Mayor Fiorello La Guardia's 1944 commission on 'marihuana', as it was then spelled.

The question for any observant and informed person must remain – knowing what we know, and having the reasonable suspicions and the correlations which we do have, would any of us knowingly permit anyone whom we loved to risk taking this drug? The only rational answer is 'No'. In which case, a strict and well-enforced law on the question would surely be a help to parents and teachers trying to keep the young away from cannabis. To say (for example) 'no, I can't risk being barred from the profession I want to follow', 'I can't risk being denied entry to the USA', or just 'I can't risk going to prison' would be an unanswerable argument against pressure to smoke cannabis. Far more than any parental warning, it would be a powerful counter to the strong peer-pressure which teenagers – who are frighteningly conformist – come under. But this could only happen if the law were enforced by both police and courts, as it has not been for decades.

---

[3] The Indian Hemp Commission of 1893–4.

4

The real purpose of classification – a better image for cannabis

The law has failed to deter, because since the Cabinet decision of February 1970, which we will examine, it has been severely weakened. From that time the law has no longer really intended to discourage the use of any illegal drugs. It has been particularly weak against cannabis, because that drug has been given a special official status which suggests to users that it is in some way 'safer' or 'softer' than other illegal drugs. As we shall see, cannabis has, from time to time, been reclassified from 'B' to 'C' and back to 'B'. But each of these changes has owed far more to politics than to science. In any case, the significant part of the classification is the implication that – officially – cannabis is less risky than the bogeymen of the narcotic world, the Class 'A' substances such as heroin, LSD and cocaine. The truth, if ever we find it out for certain, is more likely to be that cannabis carries a greater risk of irreversible damage than heroin or cocaine, and is at least as dangerous to the user's mental health as LSD, if not more so.

And so, in Britain, the ills and crimes associated with drugs have *followed* the de facto legalisation of the use and possession of formerly illegal drugs four decades ago. It is possible to argue about whether these unpleasant features of our society are caused by this decriminalisation. They may simply have happened after it, and for other reasons. But it is impossible to argue that all these bad things *result* from an illegal status these drugs do not really possess, or a prohibition which exists only in theory. And it is impossible to argue that these unpleasant effects will be diminished by making such drugs openly, instead of covertly, legal.

Such a technical change would merely formalise the arrangements which already exist. The abandonment of an unenforced law is unlikely to lead to any major social changes.

In some cases, as I argue above, the price of enforcing the law remains a matter of moral choice. Like all such choices, it involved the acceptance of some unpleasant consequences as the price of an agreed aim. Do we think the use of these drugs is wrong? Do we think that the law can be effective in limiting their use? My answer to both these questions is 'yes'. The crucial moral and cultural divide, which is at the heart of the debate about drugs, lies here. I believe self-stupefaction is absolutely morally wrong, for reasons which I set out below. My opponents, for reasons I hope I have explained, do not share this basic belief. This difference, not a chemical formula or a medical research paper, is what actually lies at the core of this debate.

The state has intervened forcefully in the sale, promotion and use of another dangerous substance, tobacco. Very few people now regard this intervention as wrong. Yet this has not always been so. As might be expected when the substance under attack is a valued pleasure among many, there was resistance to the evidence against it for many years – comparable to the cannabis lobby's current resistance to laws against their drug of choice.

The history of this dispute really goes back to the 1930s, when scientists in Hitler's Germany suggested a link between cigarettes and lung cancer. Because of the time and place of their discovery, it was ignored outside the Third Reich and forgotten after 1945. Yet it would not be long before the war that Hitler started caused the world's medical authorities to reconsider this connection. Cigarettes offer solace and comradeship in wartime (their widespread use in Britain began during the Boer War). Many more people smoked at the end of World War Two than had done so before. And it was when Richard Doll and his colleagues, worried by the large increase in lung cancer in post-war Britain, began looking for an epidemiological explanation, that the connection was first suspected, then believed likely and finally established beyond reasonable doubt.

The popularity of smoking had risen enormously in wartime, especially among women. Many people were taking up the habit, and those who had been smokers in peacetime now smoked more. The *Daily Mail* of 13 August 1941 recorded a huge wartime increase in cigarette consumption. It suggested that the heavy bombing of British cities which began in September 1940 had contributed to a 50 per cent increase in demand.

Doll and his co-workers quickly concluded that the connection between tobacco and lung cancer was inescapable. He and most of the other researchers gave up smoking themselves, long before the link was officially accepted. Although it was quite clear to most impartial observers by the middle of the 1950s that smoking was a grave danger to health, a long propaganda war continued for years afterwards, with the argument that correlation was not causation being prominent. This was an alliance between producers and consumers, both having their own strong reasons for wishing the truth was otherwise.

As late as 7 March 1962, the Tobacco Manufacturers' Standing Committee – reacting to the release of 'Smoking and Health' by the Royal College of Physicians – had the nerve to argue 'There is a growing body of evidence that smoking has pharmacological and psychological effect that are of real value to smokers'.

'The main unspoken lessons of the report are the need for far more intensive research and that only a minority of even heavy smokers get lung cancer or chronic bronchitis.'

Using an argument that would be advanced for some time to come, they even suggested that the cause of lung cancer lay elsewhere. They said 'There is increasing evidence that air pollution has a strong effect on the incidence of lung cancer, varying between given areas, and more research is needed here'.

'It has not been possible to identify the substances in tobacco smoke that might be injurious to health'.[1]

Soon afterwards Mr. C. W. Mason, chairman of Gallaher, makers of the famous and popular brand of cigarettes, Senior Service, said, 'Excess in most habits is harmful but the great majority of smokers exercise moderation in this habit from which they derive pleasure and comfort without injury to their health'.[2]

A few weeks earlier, Ted Leather, the Conservative MP for North Somerset, called the Royal College of Physicians' report, which warned of the dangers of smoking, 'unscientific tosh'. He dismissed as 'hysterical nonsense' Lord Hailsham's speech endorsing the report and calling for action. He added: 'I have every intention of enjoying my smoking until the day I die, as my grandfather did – and he lived to 95' (Mr Leather, as it happened, died aged 85).

There were, perhaps incidentally, then many Imperial Tobacco workers in his North Somerset constituency.

---

[1] Reported in the *Daily Express* of 8 March 1962.
[2] *The Guardian*, 1 May 1962.

Lord Hailsham had said the government could not be influenced by fears of lost revenue. He had called the official attitude of the tobacco industry: 'one of agnosticism bolstered up by scientific doubt'.

Also reacting to the report, Lord Sinclair of Cleeve (President of Imperial Tobacco) said in the House of Lords: 'Manufacturers have never said that heavy cigarette smoking can in no circumstances cause the disease.[3] But they do claim that to say smoking causes lung cancer is not proven'.

We hear in this argument a strong echo of today's cannabis promoters.

Several peers followed Lord Sinclair in calling attention to the supposed 'danger of air pollution', an alleged alternative explanation for increased incidence of lung cancer, long peddled by the tobacco industry's defenders. They cited as evidence for their belief the lower lung cancer death rate in the Irish Republic, where the air was much cleaner.

Meanwhile, the Tobacco Manufacturers were still claiming that smoking was on balance good for smokers, providing excuses that may have caused many men and women to delay – with tragic effects – their own abandonment of smoking. Allegedly, it was 'an aid to concentration'. It reduced tension 'particularly in emotionally stressful situations'. They also suggested that 'hyper-tension occurred less frequently in smokers than in non-smokers'. A laboratory was to be built in Harrogate for an 'extensive programme of research'.

Using the typical pro-tobacco arguments of the time, Chapman Pincher asserted that 'cigarette risks are being exaggerated'.[4] He mocked medical warnings as 'woe-woe' and maintained that the lung cancer increase was more apparent than real.

---

[3] Lung cancer.
[4] 17 March 1962, *Daily Express*, 'Why Pick on Smoking?'

All these arguments have their parallels in the cannabis lobby's current efforts to minimise the dangers of that drug.

This outbreak of hostilities was a renewal of a controversy that had in fact begun some years before. Once again, it shows that a seriously dangerous substance can remain on sale because irresponsible and/or ill-informed people, with commercial or personal interests in the matter, are prepared to argue irresponsibly or ignorantly against it, in public and often at the highest level. And they are taken seriously.

On 17 February 1954 Iain Macleod, Minister of Health, made one of the earliest government statements warnings about smoking. On 25 June that year Richard Doll declared that there was an 'association' between smoking and cancer of the lung. But the realisation that a grave and undoubted danger existed took years to have its full effect, and was vigorously resisted by both producers and users of cigarettes.

On 18 May 1956, the *Daily Mail* produced details of the early epidemiological research, recounting that Professor Bradford Hill and Dr Richard Doll had recorded lung cancer death increases following the great increase in smoking during the war years. Deaths from this cause had risen from 5,331 men and 1,237 women in 1944 to 14,820 men and 2,451 women in 1955.

They continued:

Does the statistical evidence provide a proof that cigarette smoking directly causes cancer of the lung?

No. It permits one only to deduce the most probable and reasonable interpretation.

They emphatically did not conclude that, because correlation is not causation, the connection could be ignored: 'We ourselves believe that the accumulated evidence today is such as to denote a cause and effect relationship'.

Yet despite the increasingly irresistible evidence, many educated people still preferred not to believe in a connection. On 31 October 1957, the Glasgow *Herald* reported that a suggestion by a doctor – that smoking had killed George VI – had been 'ridiculed' by the King's friends.[5]

There were also various desperate and incredible claims, similar to the arguments for 'medical marijuana' and 'self-medication' used by today's cannabis lobby. On 1 March 1959 the nation read of Dr C. N. Smyth, of University College Medical School, who claimed to have discovered a 'safe' method of smoking. His solution? Prick two holes in the cigarette with a pin.

'It is no crank theory', he proclaimed, reasonably fearing that many would think it was. It certainly does not seem to have endured.

By January 1963, it was no longer just lung cancer that was involved. A team of British doctors were reported to have started an 'all-out investigation' into links between smoking and heart disease. It is now hard to believe that the link, now undoubted, was unsuspected so recently.

But there was still resistance, on the familiar grounds of arguments set out in John Stuart Mill's essay 'On Liberty',[6] and much employed by today's cannabis lobby. When a speaker at the conference of the Co-operative Party proposed that smoking should be treated like sexually transmitted diseases, a Mr Bill Gilman, delegate from Essex, retorted grandiosely 'You are getting to the state where you are trying to interfere with the liberty of the individual'.[7]

Respectable people continued to cite the name of liberty to fight for the freedom to die young in horrible pain, leaving one's spouse

---

[5] It is now of course conventional wisdom that the King's death was accelerated by heavy smoking.
[6] 1859.
[7] 16 April 1963.

and children bereft – just as today's cannabis advocates campaign for the freedom to consign oneself to the locked ward of the mental hospital and desolate one's family. They never ceased to claim that the scientific evidence against smoking was weak. In November 1967, the Conservative MP Edward Taylor accused Kenneth Robinson, the Health Minister, of 'acting on a hunch' by ending cigarette cut-price coupon schemes.

As late as 24 October 1968, Sir George Godber, Chief Medical Officer of the Health Department, complained of 'incessant propaganda in support of cigarettes'.

On 7 January 1971, a report by the Health Education Council emphasised tobacco's dangers yet again. But six months later a rival report from the 'Tobacco Research Council'[8] claimed that cigarettes could help combat 'stress'. (Again, this is similar to the medically spurious claims of 'medical marijuana'.) It stated, irrelevantly, 'Smokers are more self-reliant and extrovert than non-smokers', a fact which might well be true, but made no difference to the dangers of lung cancer and heart disease if so. The TRC was of course financed by the cigarette industry.

By the same date, manufacturers were reported to be ready to put warnings on cigarette packets and to stop cinema advertising aimed at the young, but only under certain conditions. (They still felt strong enough to offer these actions as concessions.) They would only act if the government ignored a demand from the Royal College of Physicians for a total ban on cigarette advertising.

It is almost incredible to record that as recently as 28 November 1971, more than a decade after the danger was clear, the *Observer* reported that the Swedish Institute of Public Health had suggested

---
[8] 25 June 1971.

that some people might be able to smoke with little risk to their health.

The arguments of the tobacco lobby, as it retreated, beaten, from the field but still unwilling to admit it was wrong, are astonishing to us – yet they are similar in their moral and scientific stupidity to arguments being advanced today by the cannabis lobby. Such people would laugh at any campaign to sanitise cigarettes, but are prepared to do public relations work for cannabis.

There was, as there is now over cannabis, modest caution on the part of those doing research – even though that research would eventually turn out to be devastatingly right. The advocates of doing nothing, as they do now, chanted that correlation was not causation, or that the substance under discussion was in fact good for those who used it. And they argued, as they do now, that our freedom was threatened by legal restrictions on the habit in question. They seriously suggested that lung cancer was not caused by smoking, but by air pollution – much as the cannabis lobby argues that the connection between their favourite drug and mental illness is accidental. They claimed that tobacco could be smoked safely, just as cannabis campaigners do now. Most absurdly of all, they suggested that cigarettes actually possessed health benefits, as the 'medical marijuana' campaign does today, and as do those who say that mentally ill people smoking cannabis are 'self-medicating', and that the drug is not the cause of their illness, but a palliative for it.

These arguments do not sound quite so appealing to the fashionable, liberal voices of the cannabis lobby, when they hear them from the nicotine-scented lips of 1950s Tory MPs, Lord Beaverbrook's *Daily Express* and the hired publicists of Imperial Tobacco. Yet they ought to recognise that these people were, essentially, saying the same as they are saying now.

5

No use appealing to God. Try John Stuart Mill?

I recognise that in our secular society, an appeal to the authority of Mount Sinai or the Holy Trinity is not likely to be decisive. Many modern-minded people honestly believe that in our era all may do as they wish with their own bodies, regardless of the consequences. Some believe that the taking of drugs creates no victims, and therefore cannot be a crime. Some actually assert that the liberty to damage one's own brain and confuse one's senses is a freedom to be defended alongside the freedom of speech and thought. It is perhaps hard to see how anyone who valued either speech or thought should wish to spread the use of a drug that fuddles thought and makes speech halting and incoherent, but it is so.

Many of the advocates of drug decriminalisation (Frances Cairncross of the *Economist* being one of the most notable) rely on John Stuart Mill's 'On Liberty'. They cite its assertion that the individual is sovereign over his own mind and body as the basis for their view. Ms Cairncross wrote:

> At *The Economist*, we have always shared the view of John Stuart Mill, whose famous essay 'On Liberty' argued that a person should

be allowed to harm himself, as long as he did no harm to others. 'Over himself, over his own body and mind,' wrote Mill, 'the individual is sovereign'.[1]

Ms Cairncross, who is a CBE, and a frequent presenter of solid programmes on BBC Radio 4, has since become Rector of Exeter College, Oxford. She is a typical figure of the new liberal establishment, for whom Mill has almost scriptural force.

She used this particular quotation to back up the decision of the *Economist*, an organ of the modern British establishment, to support the decriminalisation of all drugs.

In fact, this is a questionable reading of Mill. He was arguing mainly against a highly conformist Victorian culture, the reverse of our current moral atmosphere. In any case, Mill himself got into a mess when he discussed alcohol, the only drug with which his essay dealt. He rightly rejected the monstrous and limitless idea of protecting 'social rights' under which nineteenth century prohibitionists sought a legal ban on alcohol in this country.

But after this point his essay becomes far from clear. He concedes that there are 'obvious limitations' to his maxim of leaving people to themselves: society has an 'inherent' 'right ... to ward off crimes against itself by antecedent precautions'. So it is not simply the case that 'purely self-regarding misconduct cannot properly be meddled with in the way of prevention or punishment'.

And the drug alcohol is an instance of this. Mill says

> Drunkenness, for example, in ordinary cases, is not a fit subject for legislative interference; but I should deem it perfectly legitimate that a person, who had once been convicted of any act of violence

---

[1] In the *Daily Telegraph* of 27 July 2001.

to others under the influence of drink, should be placed under a special legal restriction, personal to himself.

The offender, if he is later found drunk, 'should be liable to a penalty', and if he turns violent again, 'the punishment to which he would be liable ... should be increased in severity'.

This seems to me to be an argument about the method used by the law to intervene, not about whether the law can be mobilised in such cases. The idea of such a 'personal restriction' is not at all 'libertarian'. It resembles the Anti-Social Behaviour Orders (ASBOs) introduced – with very limited success – by the Blair government. It also (rightly) assumes that alcohol and drunkenness are already legal and endemic in our society. In this, they are unlike illegal drugs, which are a growing but far from universal scourge, still officially against the law. If alcohol is legal, we certainly cannot use the law to prevent drunkenness itself. But if alcohol were illegal (as cannabis, heroin, cocaine and ecstasy are) would Mill's objections apply? Would he have opposed the introduction of the laws which prohibited these drugs, in a period when they were very rarely used here?

By contrast, it is very hard to declare that a commonly accepted action, which has until now been legal, is against the law. Once drugs are officially and formally legalised, it is extremely difficult to make them illegal again. This is perhaps the single most important implication of current campaigns to decriminalise cannabis.

Mill concludes: 'The making himself drunk, in a person whom drunkenness excites to do harm to others, is a crime against others'.

This is true, but not true enough. Mill fails a little in imagination here. His main concern appears to be for the public violence that a drunken person may do. But the most severe effects of all drugs are not public, but private. The family of the drunkard or the drug abuser are often deeply wounded, and are among the most pitiable victims of preventable wrong in our society. The drug user may perhaps not be as violent as the drunkard. That is still open to discussion, as there are certainly instances of violent drug users. But the well-polished image of cannabis as a 'peaceful' drug is highly questionable. Many violent criminals, as well as recklessly homicidal drivers, have been found to be regular users of cannabis or under the influence of cannabis at the time of their crimes – or both.

Once again, this does not definitively identify cannabis as the reason for their violence or recklessness. But it severely undermines its carefully promoted image as a producer of calm and kindness. Probably, like any other mind-altering intoxicating drug, it removes inhibitions of all kinds. But there is also the possibility that it promotes actual irrational madness, making the user careless of the consequences of his actions, or unaware of them. In such cases, he is most likely to be a danger to himself, as was the case with Henry Cockburn. But there is a distressing number of cases of people classified as 'schizophrenic' who embark on terrible acts of random violence. It would be worth establishing how many of these individuals were cannabis users.

The cannabis user can cause terrible distress to others. He may wreck his life and the lives of his friends and close family through irreversible mental illness. He may destroy his good prospects through the other less spectacular consequences of the drug. Its use by teenagers, as many teachers well know, is associated with failure in school. Many who fail in school go on to fail in life, and so become an unquenchable grief to those who love them, and a costly burden to us all.

As the late Norman Dennis, distinguished sociologist, ethical socialist and lifelong Labour Party member, pointed out in 2003, Mill's fears of an oppressive moral climate have long ceased to be relevant:

British teenagers are now the heaviest drinkers, smokers and drug-takers in Europe. The most effective argument today for the freedom to take drugs is that it is impossible for either public opinion or the police to do anything to diminish drug-taking, and therefore the moral and legal towel should be thrown in, in defeat and despair.

That is the complete opposite to Mill's argument for liberty in 1859.

Dennis, who never in a long and distinguished life confused socialism with social liberalism, also quoted Mill's warning (in a wholly different context, but also contained in 'On Liberty') that civilisation can become 'so degenerate that neither its appointed priests or teachers, nor anybody else, has the capacity or the will to take the trouble to stand up for it'.

If Mill cannot really deal with the question of the drug user's criminal responsibility for ruining the lives of others, a more absolute code can do so. It can do so without threatening liberty in general – notably the freedoms of speech, thought and movement, and the freedom to found and maintain a family, which truly are essential to a free and civil society. All that is proposed is an effective and enforced law designed to deter vulnerable people from taking a drug whose pleasures are ultimately banal, but whose potential damage is grave.

Consider these propositions: we are responsible for ourselves and our actions; we should not reject the great gifts of the senses given to us; we should not seek to hide from ourselves the truth about the world and our society; we should not try to muffle justified discontent by blurring our minds with drugs.

If the world is at fault, and if our own lives are at fault, we must seek to change the world and our lives for the better. We should not turn our eyes, ears and minds away from the faults of the world or from our own failings.

We may be secure and wealthy in our own lives, and able to risk the ill effects of drugs, risks which fall unpredictably on some but not on others. A prominent pro-legalisation campaigner once said to me: 'I smoked cannabis and got a first at Oxford. It didn't do me any harm'. This particular person is nothing like as clever as she thinks she is, but whether that is because of the cannabis or because of plain simple vanity, I cannot know. There is of course the question, which she can never answer, of whether she might have done even better had she not taken the drug. And there is another unknowable: how can a former drug-taker measure the harm he has done to himself? That is surely up to others, who see us more clearly than we do ourselves.

But if they campaign for a reform that frees them, and 'first-class minds' like them, to take drugs, they are also campaigning for a reform that frees everyone else. That means it frees – or withdraws protection from – the beaten and rejected child of a shattered home on the squalid estate, the school failure, the unemployable young man in the post-industrial desert, the young mother living on benefits and, eventually, her children. And they are campaigning, in effect, for more people to use drugs which can, quite capriciously and unpredictably, destroy their users' mental health. So for their own convenience and peace of mind, they are willing to condemn unknown numbers of others to possible disaster. This can hardly be called a selfless action.

Finally, we are not islands. If we risk destroying ourselves (as I believe we do if we use drugs) then we risk gravely wounding those who love us and care for us. For me this is a profound individual contract. It is one that will be understood most readily by the parents of adolescent children, children who have a sort of independence but often lack the experience to use it aright. If the law makes light of those parents' concerns, and refuses to support them, what argument can they use to dissuade their young from taking a path that might well lead to permanent self-destruction? My case will I think be readily understood by the parents of children who are already destroying themselves with drugs of any kind.

6

Cannabis and violence

The following extracts from various newspapers, by no means a thorough survey or sample,[1] but striking in themselves, seem to me to be worth including in the discussion on cannabis and mental illness. Campaigners for cannabis legalisation often claim that the drug, especially in comparison with alcohol, promotes peaceful behaviour. I am unconvinced by this broad claim, partly because of the frequent newspaper accounts, such as these, of violent acts by people who are known cannabis users.

In my research, I came across a striking number of road deaths in which the driver behaved homicidally while under the influence of the drug. Government figures have shown that almost a fifth of people killed in road crashes are under the influence of drugs. But these were by no means the only instances. Here is a selection. I have included some road deaths as they occur so frequently. In some, but by no means all of these cases, cannabis has been taken together with alcohol. This is not, I believe, uncommon among cannabis users and it must remain a matter of speculation which of the two drugs had the greater influence, or whether it

---
[1] No such survey, so far as I know, has been attempted.

was the combination of the two that so destroyed the individual's inhibitions.

There are also several cases, which I have for the most part set aside, of killings by mentally ill people who have been taking cannabis. I suspect these are underestimated. These sad episodes are often not connected with cannabis at the time they are committed. It is not possible to say whether they were ill in the first place because of cannabis, or whether they were already ill for some other reason, and cannabis has made their problems worse.

> A speeding driver has been jailed after admitting he was high on cannabis when he ran over and killed a teenage girl.
>
> Landscape gardener John Page, 35, was driving a borrowed car at up to 43mph in a 30mph area in New Addington, Croydon, on June 26 last year.
>
> Lillian Groves, 14, who was playing in her front garden with her little brother, had stepped into the road to retrieve a ball when Page knocked her over. Croydon crown court heard how Page had smoked half a cannabis joint and was 'showing off' to niece Elizabeth Page and friend Gavin Timms in the car. Judge Stephen Waller said: 'There is no sentence I can pass which is going to reduce the family's pain.' Page admitted causing death by careless driving and driving without insurance. He was jailed for eight months and banned from the roads for two years.

*

> A brother and sister were behind bars last night for their part in the gang killing of a total stranger who was crippled with arthritis. Injuries inflicted on 42-year-old Gary Harper were so severe that his family were unable to recognise him.
>
> Some of his attackers, 'three who looked like children', had been

high on cannabis and Buckfast wine, the High Court in Glasgow was told.

*

High on cannabis, [Mitchell] Quy strangled his wife during one of their many blazing rows, gripping her by the neck for 20 minutes. Then, police believe, he carried out a 'ritualistic' stabbing of the body. He hid Mrs Quy's mutilated corpse for five days in the loft.

*

Fifteen minutes after leaving his family home in the Cotswolds, Jamie Waters was dead – killed in a head-on collision with a BMW driven by a man who was high on cannabis.

*

A soldier who killed a teacher in a cannabis-induced frenzy will be jailed today. Lance Corporal Laurie Draper, 31, hacked his best friend's father to death with a pair of garden shears after smoking the drug. Medical tests found he was suffering from 'cannabis induced delusions' when he attacked 53-year-old Paul Butterworth. It had been a 'nice friendly evening' until Draper smoked a joint after dinner.

*

Tom Grant, 19, was killed by a knife-wielding maniac as he travelled home from St Andrews University to see his parents. Yesterday, Thomas Wood, 22, pleaded guilty to murdering him while high on cannabis. He was sentenced to life imprisonment and the judge recommended that he serve at least 21 years ... toxicology tests on Wood after the murder showed he was high on cannabis.

*

Lee Firman, 19, stabbed Glen Corner when he intervened to help a friend who was being threatened with a knife. Jobless Firman, who was drunk and high on cannabis, stabbed him once in the chest with one of two knives he was carrying last August. He then shouted: 'I've stabbed the b*****d. Let him die.'

*

A father high on cannabis when he smothered his baby son to stop him crying was jailed for 12 years yesterday. Richard Barr, 30, from Dundee, killed one-year old Euan by putting his hand over the boy's nose and mouth and squeezing his throat, the High Court in Edinburgh was told.

Despite the efforts of paramedics and doctors, he died in Ninewell's Hospital, Dundee.

The court was told that Barr was unable to offer any explanation, but admitted having partly smothered Ewan five times before to stop him crying. Yesterday the judge, Lord Nimmo Smith, told Barr that he was lucky that his guilty plea to culpable homicide had been accepted by the Crown, as he could have faced trial for murder.

He added, however, that the sentence had to be in double figures to reflect public outrage. 'It defies comprehension that a sane person, as you appear to be, should think that an appropriate way of dealing with a crying baby is to smother him until he becomes unconscious, yet you did that on a number of occasions. You seem to have shown no awareness of how very wrong such an act was.

You were under the influence of cannabis, which may have been a factor.

*

A van driver who deliberately killed a cyclist in Islington, north London, whilst high on cannabis has been jailed for life.

Malachi Adam-Smith, 20, has smoked so much 'skunk' that he had brought on a temporary mental illness, the Old Bailey heard.

*

Two youths were imprisoned yesterday for a happy-slap killing – but will be out in months.

The two, aged 16 and 14, had faced life for attacking dad-of-two Peter Ramsey.

The younger boy slapped the 40-year-old artist as he left a store and the other, high on cannabis, punched him. Mr Ramsey fell 'like a domino' and cracked his head on the pavement.

*

The rapist was high on cannabis and ecstasy when he spotted his second victim in a Dublin park just days later.

He attacked the schoolgirl in her home and recorded the sex act on her camera phone.

I am making no claim here beyond these modest points: if cannabis is a peace-promoting drug then its effects are not always evident in its users; that I for one would be pleased to see a thorough survey done of the incidence of cannabis use among violent criminals; and that these accounts seem to me to suggest that it is reasonable to ask if cannabis might be connected with mental disturbance. We know of alcohol's association with violence, which is undoubted. But this is often cited by pro-cannabis lobbyists as a reason to prefer, or at least give equal freedom to, cannabis. But what if both drugs, taken by people morally capable of severe violence, make them more likely to commit such violence?

7

What about alcohol and tobacco, then?

This raises the question of alcohol, a horribly damaging and dangerous drug which – being legal – devastates the lives of millions. If alcohol had recently been invented and was as widely used as cannabis is now in our society, I would support the most severe legal measures to penalise its use and drive it out of our society. But this is not the case. Alcohol is too well-established here for such measures to work. A key part of this debate is involved here. Once a substance is legalised, it is extremely difficult to declare that it is illegal. That is why we should be so careful about legalising cannabis and other currently illegal drugs. If this turns out to be a mistake, it will not easily be put right.

Other means – strong restrictions on sales to minors, licensing hours and high (but not impossibly high) taxation – have worked to some extent to limit the damage that alcohol does. Interestingly, the era which has seen the growing acceptance of illegal drugs has also seen the dismantling of restrictions on alcohol in Britain. That, in my view, is the result of the same move away from responsibility and self-restraint, and towards hedonism and self-indulgence.

When pro-cannabis lobbyists have sought to challenge me by saying (as they so often do) 'What about alcohol, then?', I have found that they have fallen silent when – far from temporising, as they hoped I would do – I have challenged them to support my campaign for the return of strict licensing laws. Many are actually shocked when I suggest that the USA's experiment with prohibition of alcohol, though foredoomed, was not wholly bad. Sometimes they end the exchange by denouncing me as a 'puritan', a charge I feel increasingly ready to accept with pride.

They would not support the restrictions which I advocate, because they are hedonists who reject the Christian (and old-fashioned socialist) view of man's proper relationship to his senses. They use the alcohol problem to confuse the argument, not because they care in the slightest about the horrors of drunkenness. I suspect that most of them drink quite heavily too.

It is now forgotten that the great campaigns against alcohol in Britain, which were highly effective, originated among Christians and ethical socialists. The state was, for much of this period, neutral or in favour of widespread unrestricted alcohol sales. The importance of abstinence and teetotalism in the Labour movement is now almost entirely forgotten. But it died quite recently. The long slide into personal disaster of the fictional Labour MP Johnnie Byrne, in Wilfred Fienburgh's wrongly neglected 1959 novel *No Love for Johnnie*, begins when he defies his Temperance upbringing and drinks his first glass of whisky.

The Temperance campaigners, as I do, valued self-discipline, strong, free families, personal responsibility and clarity of the senses. Their opponents, like the drug legalisers of today, confuse pleasure, generally achieved through self-indulgence, with happiness, often the consequence of gratification deferred by duty and hard work.

The argument about drugs is one of the most important aspects of the moral and cultural revolution. It is not only about drugs, but about the abandonment of a specifically Protestant Christian way of life.

Advocates of the decriminalisation of cannabis (who will no doubt move on to the decriminalisation of other drugs once they have won this battle) are also fond of using the word 'Prohibition' to describe legal bans on their drug of choice.

By doing so, they seek to bamboozle the ill-informed with crude propaganda. They wish to suggest that all legal restrictions on all drugs will be similar to the one event with which the word 'Prohibition' is forever linked – the failed attempt to ban alcohol in the USA in the 1920s. This is famously associated with the Chicago gang wars and films such as *The Untouchables*. Thanks to its existence in popular culture, millions of people think they know rather more about American alcohol prohibition than they actually do.

In fact this episode is highly specific, is very different from the maintenance of existing laws against drugs used by a minority, and has few general lessons for us. The measure was adopted in a unique society at a time of great social and moral ferment, caused by World War One. It was soon afterwards followed by the greatest economic collapse of modern history. Support and opposition to it were linked to religious factions, classes and ethnic groups. Beer-drinking German-Americans and wine-drinking Italian-Americans, particularly, saw themselves as being picked on by puritanical Anglo-Saxon Protestants.

It took place in a country with vast unpoliced internal spaces and with two long and unenforceable borders with neighbours who permitted the sale of alcohol. And it never sought to ban the possession or consumption of alcoholic drinks, only their sale, manufacture and transport. This central weakness was undoubtedly the result of a moral uncertainty on the part of the drafters. They willed the end, but not the means. The absence of a law against possession of alcohol was a clear sign to all Americans that legislators did not really believe in the law they put forward, or think that alcohol was invariably evil.

How could they believe that, in a decidedly Christian country, when the scriptures related that Jesus Christ himself had drunk wine at the Last Supper, and turned water into wine at the wedding in Cana of Galilee? How could they, when wine, unambiguously described in scripture, was an essential part of the central ceremony of the Christian religion?

American alcohol prohibition is an interesting episode, not least because of the improvements in general health which followed it. The involvement of early feminists in this movement, such as the redoubtable Carrie Nation, is also confusing for those who wish to portray it as reactionary or repressive. In any case, a long-ago attempt to ban legal alcohol in a society wholly different from ours tells us nothing about the rights and wrongs of maintaining and strengthening Britain's existing laws against cannabis and other illegal drugs.

Britain's 1915 licensing laws, introduced on the pretext of keeping munitions workers sober in wartime, were far more effective in restricting alcohol consumption than the American Prohibition law. This was because they were cunningly timed, reinforced by a general desire to support the war effort. But it was also because their drafters recognised that alcohol was so much part of the national culture that an outright ban would never gain acceptance. So they aimed lower and hit their mark. Drunkenness and its invariable, gaunt companions – wife-beating, child neglect and cruelty to children, street disorder, disease, absence from work – were much reduced. These effects continued until the 1980s when the laws were relaxed in pursuit of a continental 'café culture' and of the 'civilised' society sought by Anthony Crosland in his *The Future of Socialism*.[1]

---

[1] Jonathan Cape, 2006.

Likewise, Scandinavia's severe restrictions on alcohol sales, accompanied by heavy taxes, have been far more successful in reducing drinking than the near-prohibition introduced by Mikhail Gorbachev in the dying years of the USSR. President Gorbachev's laws mainly resulted in a severe shortage of sugar, as Russians used their bathtubs to make 'Samogon' moonshine.

Similarly, it is perfectly possible to obtain alcohol in the Islamic Republic of Iran, one of the most repressive states on Earth, despite a supposed total prohibition there. Persian culture, like that of Christian Europe, has permitted alcohol for thousands of years. Persia's great poets, who in many cases praise wine, mostly wrote before Islamic propriety sought to stamp it out. The modern Islamic ban was imposed on a society which had for centuries regarded alcohol – for good or ill – as civilised, permissible and legal. Once again, it is not comparable with laws against drugs such as cannabis, which were almost unknown in Britain until the early 1960s, and are still viewed in this country with widespread and justified suspicion.

That is why what is true of alcohol simply is not true of cannabis, cocaine, heroin or 'ecstasy'. But it is, interestingly partly true of tobacco. Efforts to discourage cigarette smoking, cunningly devised and backed by insistent and clever propaganda from school upwards, have been surprisingly effective. This is partly because mass cigarette smoking is in fact very recent in Western culture, having grown up mainly during two wartime periods in the twentieth century. It is also because of an unchallengeable scientific certainty that cigarette smoking promotes several horrible diseases. I suspect it is greatly helped by the fact that non-smokers generally find smoking rather disgusting, especially near food, and that fire insurance premiums fall sharply in buildings where smoking is banned. Despite the fact that it is a very difficult habit to break, millions have done so.

Generally, the better-educated and more prosperous have been more successful. But there is no doubt that it is a habit that is in retreat in this country. Many measures have been taken to achieve this. Sales and advertising have been restricted, and taxes levied, but it is the act of lighting and smoking the cigarette itself which has been most besieged by legal restrictions.

This has worked, just as the cannabis law, which since 1971 has concentrated entirely on supply and ignores advertising, possession and use, has not worked. The anti-cigarette law has also placed a legal obligation on the owners of premises to prevent the lighting and smoking of tobacco. This has worked, just as the cannabis law, which ceased to penalise the owners of premises used for smoking that drug after 1971, has not worked.

Another law aimed directly at behaviour and personal use of a drug has also been highly effective. This is the law which punishes drunken driving. Once again, the individual's actual consumption has been made subject to law, through the breathalyser. Both these examples, of the campaign to reduce smoking and the effort to reduce drunken driving, provide absolute proof that a consistently and energetically applied law, directed at users of a drug, can sharply reduce its use. The courts and prisons are not full of transgressors. Instead, the incidence of these things has decreased.

It is curious to contrast these expensive and intensive campaigns with the official attitude towards cannabis and other illegal drugs. Officials encourage schools and other publicly funded bodies to issue propaganda which accepts that young people are bound to take drugs (thus making drug taking more likely). Much of this material also suggests (falsely) that there are 'safe' ways of consuming drugs. The website 'Talk to Frank' is typical of this form of jaunty appeasement. By contrast, the Government has always scornfully dismissed the tobacco companies' attempts to produce a 'safe' or 'safer' cigarette. It has said many times (and rightly) that the habit is invariably a danger. It has greatly exaggerated the dangers of second-hand smoke to make general bans in shops, offices, pubs and restaurants more acceptable. It does not treat habitual smoking as an intractable disease whose sufferers are passive victims to be pitied and offered slightly less dangerous substitutes for their drug of choice, as it does with heroin. It spends a great deal of money on various therapies whose only aim is to help the smoker to give up for good.

Meanwhile there is strong social disapproval of public figures who smoke, and even more so of private individuals who do so. The contrast between the two government attitudes is striking. One possible explanation is that the British National Health Service, once described by Lord (Nigel) Lawson, as the closest thing which Britain now has to a religion, is severely burdened by the effects of smoking on health. Smoking is therefore a sin against the NHS, a sin against the sovereign people, and universally considered to be bad. Perhaps, if the connection between cannabis and mental illness is eventually recognised, a similar attitude will arise.

I think it is fair to say, in the light of these facts, that the current campaign for legalisation, or what is euphemistically described as 'regulation', of some illegal drugs is based either upon grave ignorance of the issues, or upon deliberate dishonesty.

My own belief is that the advocates of this change are either gullible and ill-informed (the majority), or that they actively wish to permit the legal commercial exploitation of the undoubted demand for stupefying drugs. In some cases, they may even wish to raise tax revenues from such drugs. Those who speak on these matters might usefully be asked if they have any material interest in the effects of 'regulation'.

8

The Cabinet gets it wrong

'Drug law shock', read the front page of the *Sunday Mirror*, on 1 February 1970. 'Jim Changes His Mind. Penalties for Pot Smokers to be Cut'. The 'Jim' was the Home Secretary James Callaghan; what the *Sunday Mirror* did not mention was that it was Callaghan who had leaked the story to the newspaper. What was the shock, and why did Callaghan go to the press?

February 1970 was a decisive moment of decriminalisation. And thanks to that rather louche and radical politician, troublemaker and diarist, Richard Crossman, we have a first-hand (if partial) account of the Cabinet meeting which led to a change in the law, alongside the bald Cabinet minutes.

Crossman recorded in his diaries[1] the telling fact that – on this issue – a Labour cabinet divided on class lines, between the socially conservative working class members, and the socially radical university graduates who were increasingly taking over the party. It was one of the most momentous decisions taken by that revolu-

---

[1] *The Crossman Diaries* 1964–70, Jonathan Cape, London 1979, p.613, one-volume edition.

tionary government, and has since reached deep into the lives of millions. Yet while it divided the senior ranks of the Labour Party, it did not divide a British establishment which was already far more radical on such issues than is generally realised.

Take, for instance the fascinating history of Henry Bryan Spear, known to his friends as 'Bing', who became chief inspector of the Dangerous Drugs Branch of the Home Office in 1977 and held that post for nine years. He was described in his obituary in *The Times* as 'a friend to many heroin addicts on the London streets in the 1960s and 1970s'. He used his considerable influence to steer national drug policy towards appeasement and containment of drug taking, rather than punitive eradication. He joined the (then tiny) Dangerous Drugs Branch of the Home Office in 1952. As *The Times* noted, drug abusers in those days numbered only 'a few hundred, with the problems centring on musicians, a few seamen and some members of the medical profession'.

By the time he retired in 1986 the number of heroin abusers ran into tens of thousands. Mr Spear cannot of course be personally blamed for this. As his obituarist rightly pointed out, 'the 1960s had created the culture of the recreational drug, and few towns or cities in Britain could claim to be free of drug abuse'. But he can be blamed for helping it to get worse, and missing an opportunity to halt it.

It was not fore-ordained that the 1960s drug culture would continue to expand unchallenged. Nor would the level of drug abuse necessarily have remained so high or continued to grow if a different policy had been followed. Sweden, for example, has taken a very different path and has less drug abuse than much of the rest of the continent. These facts may possibly be connected. These matters were not beyond the influence of government, police and courts. A senior permanent official who believed in accommodation and 'treatment' rather than in deterrence was well positioned to make a great difference.

Spear's view is clear from his behaviour and his associates. He knew many addicts as friends. In an obituary of Rufus Harris, co-founder of the drug legalisation campaign group 'Release', the veteran campaigner for drug law relaxation, Steve Abrams, noted,

> From 1967 onwards, Rufus maintained a contact with the legendary head of the Home Office Drugs Inspectorate, H. B. 'Bing' Spear, who was at the centre of all progressive developments in the field. Rufus was an honours graduate of what Arnold Trebach, founder of the Drug Policy Foundation, called the 'Bing Spear University'. He remained in contact with Spear long after he left Release and after Spear retired from the Home Office.[2]

Bing Spear's existence and activities, had they come to the notice of the conservative media, would have attracted a great deal of interest and criticism. But they have never even heard of him. His name is not to be found in their archives. No doubt he was pleased and relieved at that. Truly effective lobbies operate quietly and without publicity, which they do not need because they have the ear of the powerful. Steve Abrams's obituary of Mr Spear also noted that the organisation 'Release', formed to help people who had been arrested for possession of illegal drugs, was initially keenly supported by the Tory politician Jonathan Aitken, then a mainstream conservative politician with a ministerial career ahead of him. These facts are simply incompatible with the fanciful but widespread belief that the British establishment is engaged in a stern war against drugs.

While there was still some debate about drug laws in the media and

---

[2] *The Guardian*, 30 April 2007.

Parliament in the late 1960s and early 1970s, the matter was already more or less settled in the minds of officials and law enforcers, as we shall see in much more detail.

This is why it is no surprise that the decision to decriminalise cannabis in all but name, achieved in February 1970 by Labour's culturally revolutionary 'progressive' wing, survived the Conservative Party's general election victory four months later.

The legislation was accepted and absorbed without amendment by Edward Heath's Tory Cabinet. It was then pushed rapidly through Parliament and into law. This fact will be surprising only to those who have not studied the history of the Conservative Party, which long ago adopted similar 'progressive' policies to those of Richard Crossman and his Cabinet allies. I have written in *The Abolition of Britain*[3] about the 'progressive' cross-party alliance formed by Roy Jenkins in the early 1960s, born out of a common desire among culturally and morally radical Labour MPs and their Tory equivalents to foster a revolutionary programme, as set out in Jenkins's *The Labour Case*,[4] and Anthony Crosland's *The Future of Socialism*, published in 1956. Its first success was the Obscene Publications Act, which led directly to the obscenity trial of D. H. Lawrence's novel *Lady Chatterley's Lover*, and eventually to the legalisation of almost all pornography. Later, it helped to pass several of the measures which created the 'Permissive' or (as Lord Jenkins preferred) 'Civilised' Society in the 1964–70 period.

Most of these changes were officially Private Members' Bills. The party whips did not demand disciplined support for them. This allowed socially conservative Labour MPs to oppose them, and socially liberal Tories to support them. But in reality, they

---

[3] Quartet, 1999.
[4] Penguin, 1959.

were far from private, having powerful government backing to get them the necessary Parliamentary time. The alliance's single most significant achievement was the approval of British membership of the European Common Market in 1972. It has, since then, formed an unofficial political formation more powerful than any of the three major parties.[5]

Its mobilisation would eventually transform the Labour Party from a socially cautious, patriotic and largely Christian coalition, based on industrial workers, into a metropolitan radical formation largely answerable to the tastes and desires of the university-educated middle class. In the Cabinet vote on cannabis, the division is unusually clear.

'It was fascinating to see', Crossman wrote, 'that at this point we had for the first time a sociological vote, that is to say every member of the Cabinet who had been at university voted one way and everyone else voted the other'. Crossman is – characteristically – slightly distorting the truth here. Harold Wilson, who despite a modest background had been at Oxford as an undergraduate and as a don, cannily voted with the working-class ministers to begin with, but then switched sides when the vote went against him.

The issue was twofold. The planned Misuse of Drugs Bill would – for the first time in Britain or the world – treat some illegal drugs, notably cannabis, as less serious than others. The main effects of this were considerable and lasting. First, it gave official support to the idea that cannabis was so much less harmful than heroin and LSD that it should be in a separate legal category. This is very hard to justify scientifically, not least because the harms done by various drugs are of totally different kinds and cannot readily be compared on the same scale. It is also morally difficult. If self-stupefaction is itself

---

[5] See my *The Cameron Delusion*, Continuum, 2010, for an examination of this.

wrong – which must be the principle behind any law controlling a stupefying drug – then surely all illegal forms of it are equally wrong.

But the authors of this law could hardly have found a better way to encourage the baseless but widespread belief that cannabis is a 'soft' drug with few if any harmful effects.

Second, it separated the offence of trafficking from the offence of possession, and made the penalties for possession alone much weaker. As we shall see, this would lead over time to the effective decriminalisation of cannabis possession.

This distinction was also to be the foundation of another key policy. From then on the state sought, with much rhetoric and rather less action, to interdict the supply of drugs, classed as an extraordinarily evil activity. Yet at the same time it viewed the use and possession of these same drugs as a minor offence. So it made almost no effort to interdict demand. Thus, in some mysterious way, the drug was evil as it flourished in the fields, evil during its long journey from grower to smuggler, and still more evil in the hands of the seller. But it became miraculously innocent at the moment when it passed to the hands of the buyer, the only one who would actually experience its effects. Yet it is presumably those effects which make the drug morally objectionable and justify its illegal status.

This inexplicable transformation of a substance from appalling wickedness to light-hearted harmlessness, at the moment of sale, makes the Roman Catholic belief in the transubstantiation of bread and wine into the flesh and blood of Christ seem a relatively undemanding concept. Yet it takes place between normal men and women, without ceremony or apostolic succession, hundreds of times each day at school gates, on street corners and in pubs, and nobody marvels about it at all.

The proposed Bill also greatly reduced the drug taker's fear of informers, always an important weapon in the hands of the law when offences are being committed in private places. With maximum penalties reduced to such low levels, the police would pay little, and do few favours, to those who brought them mere possessors of drugs. It also abolished the absolute offence of allowing drugs to be used on one's premises. This removed a powerful deterrent weapon from the hands of parents and other responsible people who wished to forbid the use of drugs under their roofs. The argument 'You cannot do that here, or I might go to prison' is hard to counter.

9

Enter Richard Crossman

Crossman's account must be understood as the view of a social liberal and an actual libertine. During his pre-war years as an Oxford don, this interesting man had outraged colleagues, and destroyed a promising academic career, through his relaxed sexual morals.

Crossman, son of a Tory judge, in many ways epitomises the combination of sexual, moral and political adventurousness that pervaded Britain's intellectual left far further back in the twentieth century than most people realise. To the student generation of the late 1960s and early 1970s, the Wilson Cabinet appeared conservative and stuffy. Its members wore suits and ties, kept their hair cut short and spoke in the measured tones of upper-middle-class England. But their minds were as radical as those of any flower child. Many of them had extremely radical micro-politics, often connected to adventurous sexual lives.

Crossman is an excellent example of this. As an undergraduate, he is thought to have conducted an affair with Stephen Spender. As a New College don, he had another affair with Zita Baker, a married woman. Mrs Baker also aborted his baby. Later, after the affair had become public knowledge, Crossman married her. Though Crossman was obviously uncomfortable about admitting it, this was his second marriage. Crossman had divorced his first wife, the mysterious and outrageous Erika, before the affair with Zita.

The mature Crossman did not even mention Erika's existence in his entry in *Who's Who*, 30 years later. He said he had been married only twice (he had married for the third and last time after Zita's death). Perhaps this is precisely because Erika had a major influence on his life and attitudes, and on his politics. At one stage she introduced him to the notorious Communist propagandist Willi Münzenberg, who promptly recognised his qualities and tried to persuade him to go to work for Stalin in Moscow. Crossman had more sense than to accept. The interesting thing is that Münzenberg thought it worth asking.

In a letter to Zita during their affair, Crossman described them both as 'modern unconventionals'. This was not the only way in which he proved himself unconventional, by the standards of his own youth and of those who came many years afterwards. He famously perjured himself in 1957, lying on oath that he had not been drunk at a conference in Italy, after the *Spectator* magazine had published an article correctly saying that he had been. As a result he was paid substantial damages. This behaviour, lying for money while trying to conceal a drunken episode from voters who would not approve of it, illustrates two more ways in which he might have been less straitlaced than he appeared.

It would be wrong to attribute Crossman's moral attitudes to the entire Labour intellectual hierarchy. But it would be fair to say that most of them would have been happy with the label 'modern unconventionals', and – like many of their equivalents today – would have seen nothing very wrong in a little self-stupefaction. But they would not have wanted to say so in public.

It is not surprising that Crossman's account drips scorn upon the behaviour of the Home Secretary, James Callaghan. Callaghan was by contrast prosaic and far from liberal. He had for many years been the official spokesman of the Police Federation in the House of Commons. His father, a Royal Navy Petty Officer, had died when he was young. He could not afford to go to university despite gaining the Senior Oxford Certificate from his Portsmouth council school, so entered a lowly branch of the civil service to earn a living. He served in the Royal Navy during the Second World War. (Richard Crossman spent the war working, appropriately enough, on black propaganda.)

Callaghan remained faithful all his life to his wife Audrey – whom he had met when they were both Sunday School teachers at a Maidstone Baptist church. The patrician, bohemian Crossman was an intellectual snob of some distinction. He had little in common with this respectably suburban former tax clerk and insignificant union official, except that he belonged to the same political party and the same Cabinet. Callaghan was a representative of all the things Crossman most disliked about his own party – and it is common in British politics for more elevated figures to be more hostile to their own party than to their formal opponents.

At the time he wrote his diary entry for that day, Crossman was planning to leak the private thoughts of an entire government when the moment was right. So when he complains of Callaghan's responsibility for the 'absolutely outrageous' leak to the *Sunday Mirror*, it is impossible to take him seriously. Crossman was in no position to be angry about other people's leaks, and he knew it. He was annoyed about Callaghan's views, not about his behaviour.

He summed up the leak as saying that 'Callaghan had been overruled and that the Government was going to go soft on drugs and make major concessions on cannabis'. Crossman comments 'This was very awkward because it wasn't quite true'. Yet the *Sunday Mirror* story was perfectly true.

It began:

Home Secretary James Callaghan has had a dramatic change of mind on drugs. He has decided that people who smoke pot should no longer be punished as severely as those using heroin. He has gone further by proposing that the penalties for possessing both hard and soft drugs should be cut ... Mr Callaghan only a year ago championed the cause of holding the line against drug permissiveness ... last year Mr Callaghan denounced what he called 'a notorious advertisement' in The Times – signed by many public figures including the Beatles – which urged that possessing cannabis should either be legalised, or at most punishable by a fine of not more than £25.

It is not clear whether Callaghan was really being overruled by his Cabinet colleagues, though it seems likely that the leak was a cunning way of creating a newspaper storm and reversing the decision. It is possible that he had genuinely changed his mind.

In either case, the leak was wholly justified by what had actually happened. The effect of the planned legislation was greatly to weaken the laws against drugs. And it is hard to see what other purpose the changes could have had. This weakening of the law had also been the intention of the Wootton Committee. Their report – completed in 1968, reluctantly published by Callaghan in early 1969 – had been drafted in response to the 'notorious advertisement' (discussed at length in later chapters). Their deliberations had been heavily influenced by the cannabis lobby and their findings were the basis of the new Bill. Callaghan (as we shall see) had denounced the report when it was first published, and it was even suggested that he had attempted to prevent its publication.

Crossman argues that the real division on that day was not over principle, but over the government's fear of public opinion. He writes as if an intelligent Cabinet would naturally have wanted a progressive liberal measure, as he did. Having made up his own mind, he assumes that its more conservative members had no actual argument against liberalisation but were motivated only by cowardice and a feeble, unprincipled fear of the voters. This seems unlikely, given the chapel-influenced, temperance-minded and generally puritan background of working-class Labour, especially in Wales and Scotland.

Such people would have instinctively viewed the taking of drugs with unfeigned disapproval. More believable is the idea that the dissenters – Callaghan himself, Edward Short, William Ross, Roy Mason, Fred Peart, George Thomson, Cledwyn Hughes and George Thomas – thought it pointless to argue on principle. They knew well that the university-educated radicals were from another world.

Did they instead try to dissuade the radicals by warning that the change might help lose the fast-approaching general election? It was certainly the best argument they had that morning. Everyone knew the election would be soon, and would be close. But whatever their intentions, the attempt narrowly failed. Those in favour of drug liberalisation were Gerald Gardiner, Barbara Castle, Denis Healey, Anthony Crosland, Roy Jenkins, Crossman himself, Peter Shore, Lord Shackleton, Tony Benn (then known as Anthony Wedgwood Benn), Jack Diamond and Harold Lever. As Crossman puts it 'We were all progressives'.

The Cabinet minutes[1] do not solve the puzzle of what the dissenting minority's real objections were. But they do set out the impossibly garbled thinking enshrined in the Bill (and in all British government action on the subject ever since). They note:

But if – as was clearly right – the penalties for trafficking should

---

[1] CC70, 10th Conclusions, pp.10–11.

be increased (e.g. in the case of the most dangerous drugs, from the existing limit of ten years' imprisonment to a new limit of 14 years), it followed that the penalties for simple possession of the less serious drugs should be reduced.

In other words, sterner punishments for trafficking mean more lenient punishments for possession. The mystery is why the minutes say that it did follow, when it so obviously did not. If drug possession is less serious, then why should trafficking of the same drugs be more serious? The logic fails in both directions. And it fails at its heart. It is the nature of the drug that makes the trafficking undesirable. If the traffickers carried and sold sugar or soap instead, they would not be committing a crime. So it is not the carrying or the selling that makes the offence, but the drug itself.

It is offensive because it is nasty and dangerous. Presumably the dangerous qualities of the drug, which are only experienced by the person who voluntarily buys, deliberately possesses and purposely uses it, are the reason for this distinction. So why is it wicked to traffic in it, but far less so to possess and use it? No explanation is offered. No reasoning behind the law is provided at all.

They continue: 'and the Committee had recommended that on this basis the penalty for the possession of cannabis might be curtailed from ten years to three years'.

This reduction would have completely transformed the nature of the offence, as maximum sentences are rarely if ever imposed. In fact, within a few years a Conservative Lord Chancellor, Lord Hailsham, would be explicitly telling magistrates to stop sending anyone to prison at all for cannabis possession.

To some extent, the social conservatives succeeded in scaring their radical colleagues. The minutes show that even the 'progressive' majority were not quite ready for the planned very sharp reduction in penalties, with a general election probably months away. The government had suffered several reverses, mainly over its failed attempt to control trade union power. It had good reason to be nervous about any radical legislation. In theory, with his large majority, Harold Wilson could have continued in office until March 1971. But waiting till the last minute to hold an election can be very dangerous, if a major problem erupts in the final few weeks of office. It had not saved the Tories from defeat in October 1964. So everyone in politics assumed that a poll in the very near future was highly likely. It did in fact take place on 18 June 1970. Labour lost, a result so unexpected by the BBC that a painter had to be called into the Corporation's election studio to extend the 'swingometer' recording the swing to the Tories.

10

Jim Callaghan's last stand

The minutes state that Callaghan put up a sort of last stand. It is impossible to be sure, at this distance, what this very subtle politician really intended. Was he seeking to dilute the radicals' plan? Or did he intend to defeat it through guile, and fail? There are strong suggestions, in most of his public remarks on the subject, that he strongly disliked the change. But in the end he did not prevent it. All we can say with certainty is that he did not choose to resign over the issue. The minutes record his concern that 'public opinion might well regard a change of this kind as indicating too lenient an attitude on the part of the Government towards the potentially dangerous practice of drug taking'. He added that this impression of leniency might cause the Government 'political damage' – by which he meant lost votes.

Callaghan advised abandoning the distinction (crucial to the reformers' scheme to give cannabis a special status) between different drugs. He urged a single, fierce maximum penalty for possession of any illegal drug (either seven or ten years in prison) and a single even higher maximum for trafficking (14 years). If these proposals had stood, the view that cannabis was a 'soft drug' would have suffered a severe reverse. And the whittling away of penalties for possession of cannabis in the years to come would have been far harder. Lord Hailsham's later instruction to magistrates to keep cannabis users out of prison would have been impossible.

But Callaghan failed to change any minds. And so the direction was now clear. The majority of the Cabinet wanted to keep the different classifications. Presumably they realised that this was an important stage in lessening the law's effectiveness against cannabis users. Some of them must certainly have hoped that it would be. But they also accepted that

> the proposed reduction of the penalty for simple possession of cannabis from ten years' imprisonment to three years would be liable to be severely criticised by public opinion, especially by parents and teachers ... It would be very unwise to underestimate the degree of public concern on this subject and the ease with which the government's intentions might be misinterpreted'.[1]

Or perhaps, the minutes might more truthfully have warned of the ease with which the government's 'progressive' and liberalising intentions might have been correctly interpreted. As it happened, the change went ahead without any significant opposition. The public and the media would be preoccupied with other subjects – strikes, inflation, the European Common Market and rising oil prices – for years to come. The moral and cultural revolution would become so quiet during the mid-1970s that many came to believe it had ceased.

When the Bill eventually came before Parliament, nobody noticed its genuinely radical aims and effects. As is so often the case in drugs debates, dim and ill-informed conservatives mistook rhetoric for

---

[1] Cabinet minutes CC70 10th – Conclusions pp.10–11.

reality, while liberals continued to claim that the law was too harsh. Media debate, which was rare, continued along the same banal lines.

The British government had chosen an approach which continues to the present. It would quietly shift the law in a radical direction, while doing all it could to maintain the pretence that it was stern and diligent in keeping young people safe from dangerous drugs. As we shall see, this would be done by the salami-slicing process, each stage so small that opponents either could not recognise it for what it was, or could not rally enough opposition to prevent it. As we shall also see, by 2007, the bulk of cannabis possession cases that the police even troubled to record would be dealt with by a 'warning' that involved no criminal record of any kind, a long way from a maximum of ten years' imprisonment. Even possession of the supposedly more serious Class 'A' drugs would, in most cases, not result in imprisonment.

The pretence would satisfy the large part of the public which has never accepted the Cultural Revolution. It would reassure them because it appeared to be firm, and because no official declaration was made that the drug was in fact being decriminalised in stages. But it would achieve this without actually causing much inconvenience to the drug users. They in their turn have helped the state appear decisive and 'tough', by continuing to complain about how persecuted they are. This process, known to American political professionals as 'Triangulation', allows political figures and parties to define themselves against carefully chosen opponents, rather than through concrete actions. It deals in appearance, not in fact.

It would also – and this is very important in this process – avoid any direct breach of Britain's international treaty obligations, which compel Her Majesty's Government to enact and maintain laws against these particular drugs. The mystery would be 'Why is all this "toughness" having so little effect?' The answer of the legalisers would be 'Because prohibition does not work'. It was not in the interest of the government or the legalisers to admit the truth – that the 'toughness' was faked, and could not work because it did not actually exist.

This approach explains – as nothing else can – the bizarre logic of creating three classes of drug. To this day, the scientific basis for these classifications is elusive. The harms associated with heroin are quite different from those linked with cocaine. And those associated with cannabis are different from either of these. Cannabis appears to be linked to a threat to mental health which the others do not share. But the physical dangers of heroin and cocaine (while different from each other) are markedly greater than the physical risks of cannabis. This hardly justifies the use of the word 'soft' to describe cannabis. In this context, the expression calls to mind its only other comparable use – to describe 'soft' drinks such as lemonade and colas. But 'soft' drinks are so called not because they are milder than 'hard' drinks, but because they are completely non-alcoholic. They are absolutely distinct from hard liquor or even from milder alcoholic beverages such as weak beer and cider.

Cannabis, by contrast, is a powerful mind-altering drug which is increasingly correlated with serious mental illness. Whatever the faults of sweet, fizzy non-alcoholic drinks, their risks are not remotely like those of cannabis. The designation is completely misleading, yet the British state's system of drug classification gives this dangerous falsehood great and lasting legitimacy.

That system is not scientific at all, but political. The classification is rightly mocked by such figures as Professor David Nutt, a supporter of further relaxation of the law. Campaigners for more effective drug laws have foolishly allowed themselves to be drawn into controversies over whether cannabis should be classified as 'B' or 'C'. They should instead have been arguing for the abolition of all classifications, which have only served to promote the idea that cannabis is not as serious as other illegal drugs.

From the moment of the Cabinet decision in February 1970, the course of events was clear. Personal use of drugs, especially cannabis, was to be tacitly permitted. Any remaining disquiet over drugs among voters was to be placated by a futile but well-publicised pursuit of suppliers.

In the pages to come, we will see many more examples of this approach in theory and practice. It is the key to understanding the course of events ever since.

The Prime Minister, Harold Wilson, accepted the small majority in favour of liberalisation, but said it

> might help to allay public disquiet if the proposed penalties for possession of controlled drugs were increased to some extent – e.g. to seven years (instead of five years) for the most serious drugs and to five years (instead of three years) for drugs in the second [My note: less serious] category, including cannabis.

He did not actually mean 'increased'. He meant 'decreased less'. The maximum sentence for possession or trafficking under the existing law[2] was ten years in prison. The 1965 Act made no distinction between possession or supply, and regarded heroin, cocaine and cannabis as equally pernicious.

Once again, while conceding unimportant ground, the 'Progressives' and 'Modern Unconventionals' held on to the crucial elements of the revolution they supported. Cannabis was to be treated as officially less dangerous than heroin or LSD. And possession, which really means use, was to be treated utterly differently from trafficking.

The Cabinet agreed that the Bill should go forward on this basis, and told the Home Secretary to introduce it in that shape. And so he did, but he never finished his task. The June 1970 General Election

---

[2] The Dangerous Drugs Act 1965, itself a revised version of a 1920 law.

sent James Callaghan into Opposition for the next four years. He would never be Home Secretary again.

It is interesting to reflect, given the strange, lingering belief that Conservative Governments are substantially different from Labour ones, that the policy was considered so uncontroversial that the new Tory government adopted it as a whole and unchanged. Jim Callaghan's Bill (perhaps to Callaghan's relief) was eventually piloted through Parliament by the mildly corrupt, genial, whisky-loving liberal Tory, Reginald Maudling – a libertarian Oxford graduate and Hegel enthusiast who had more in common with Richard Crossman than he did with James Callaghan. And he devolved much of the task to his Minister in the Lords, Lord Windlesham, a member of the Hennessy brandy family and a former TV executive. If not exactly an 'unconventional modern', Windlesham was far more relaxed on social, moral and cultural matters than Jim Callaghan ever was.

This extraordinary handover of a far-reaching Act of Parliament from one party to its supposed opponent is itself a fascinating historical detail. It illustrates once more that on issues of cultural and moral revolution, the Labour and Conservative elites had during the 1960s formed an effective alliance against their own more conservative members and supporters.

Part Two

The Search for Soma

'All the advantages of Christianity and alcohol; none of their defects'.

ALDOUS HUXLEY, *BRAVE NEW WORLD*, 1932

11

Aldous Huxley

Aldous Huxley meant his novel *Brave New World* to be a warning. To the men and women of his own time, that is what it was. But to our age it is nothing like as disturbing as it was when it was first published in 1932. Much more than its rival dystopia, George Orwell's *Nineteen Eighty Four*, it has actually come true in the years since it was written. Like Cassandra, Huxley was condemned to be right, but not to be believed. Worse, the things he sought to warn us against, which to him were obviously repellent, are actually desired by many of us today. Just as it sometimes seems that North Korea's despot, Kim il Sung, used Orwell's book as an instruction manual, many children of the modern age might well see Huxley's nightmare as an ideal and well-run version of the world in which they live.

I would here like to quote at length the extraordinary warning that Huxley later issued:[1]

> It seems to me that the nature of the ultimate revolution with which we are now faced is precisely this: That we are in process of developing a whole series of techniques which will enable the

---
[1] In a talk entitled 'The Ultimate Revolution' given at Berkeley University on 20 March 1962.

controlling oligarchy who have always existed and presumably will always exist to get people to love their servitude.

This is the, it seems to me, the ultimate in malevolent revolutions ... and this is a problem which has interested me many years and about which I wrote, thirty years ago, a fable, 'Brave New World', which is an account of society making use of all the devices available and some of the devices which I imagined to be possible making use of them in order, first of all, to standardize the population, to iron out inconvenient human differences, to create mass produced models of human beings arranged in some sort of scientific caste system. Since then, I have continued to be extremely interested in this problem and I have noticed with increasing dismay a number of the predictions which were purely fantastic when I made them thirty years ago have come true or seem in process of coming true.

A number of techniques about which I talked seem to be here already. And there seems to be a general movement in the direction of this kind of ultimate revolution, a method of control by which a people can be made to enjoy a state of affairs by which any decent standard they ought not to enjoy ... the enjoyment of servitude.

Such is the power and accuracy of Huxley's prophecy that it seems more and more like a prediction of an attainable and approaching future, less and less like a wild caricature of 1930s scientific fantasy: contraception universal, family relations in many cases abolished, all the inhibitions surrounding sex removed, an ill-educated mass kept content with (legal and illegal) drugs and with sport and entertainment, old age hidden from sight and – increasingly – ended by deliberate neglect or disguised euthanasia, death a process conducted offstage among strangers, history forgotten, Christianity reduced to community singing, reading books a quaint minority pursuit, education indoctrination, the nation state fading into oblivion, science fumbling busily in the womb, sometimes killing, sometimes manipulating.

Huxley's world is all too close to the way we live now. But there is one big thing missing. It is the element that makes Huxley's dystopia work with complete smoothness, and which we do not have. This is the mysterious drug Soma, developed (according to the novel) in six intensive years by 2,000 pharmacologists and biochemists, richly subsidised so as to produce the perfect narcotic. It is said to have 'All the advantages of Christianity and alcohol; none of their defects ... take a holiday from reality whenever you like, and come back without so much as a headache or a mythology'.

Soma silences worry, makes the unfunny funny, provides a holiday from reality. 'A gramme', all citizens are taught from birth 'is better than a damn'. As Huxley summarises it: 'There is always soma, delicious soma, half a gramme for a half-holiday, a gramme for a week-end, two grammes for a trip to the gorgeous East, three for a dark eternity on the moon ...'.

At one stage a riot is quelled with it:

> Three men with spraying machines buckled to their shoulders pumped thick clouds of soma vapour into the air ... Two minutes later the Voice and the soma vapour had produced their effect. In tears, the Deltas were kissing and hugging one another—half a dozen twins at a time in a comprehensive embrace.

Of course there is no such harmless drug. There are good reasons why there never could be. A drug that could do this in the present would exact its price in the future. But might such a thing not seem desirable, in a society devoted to consumption ('ending is better than mending'), in which the people have been distracted from culture and politics by entertainment, lotteries and consumer pleasures, and religion supplanted by celebrity worship, football and rock music?

Modern Britain long ago ceased to believe in the Kingdom of Heaven, and sought instead an earthly paradise. Tangible, immediate pleasure was to replace the means of grace and the hope of glory, and also to sweep away the discipline of patience.

The new society forsook the consolations of religion and abandoned the stern Protestant insistence on deferred gratification which had enabled it to endure the Industrial Revolution, two Great Depressions and two appalling wars. It had ceased to hide its griefs or to say 'mustn't grumble' at moments when any other country would have grumbled. Why not then take the next step and abandon ancient objections to the intoxicated state?

These objections are, after all, Jewish and Christian in origin, based upon ideas of self-discipline, self-control, guilt and sin which have been largely abandoned by our culture. The great temperance movement, the core of the alliance between Labour and Christianity, was quite dead by 1970. But for those who wanted to pursue post-Christian policies, difficulties remained. Those who had moral objections to self-stupefaction were still nominally in control of the national culture and morality.

Protestant Christianity, with its insistence on an eternal reward and its scorn for self-indulgence, was still the official religion of the nation. The law, based as it was upon such Christianity, frowned particularly on unearned pleasure, and so on the drowsy fumes of marijuana. A small, relaxed elite might find this attitude objectionable or even funny. But they knew that the long afterglow of Protestant morality still continued, and would do so for some years to come. 1970 – or 1980, or 1990 – was far too early to make an open declaration that such drugs were no longer to be subject to severe legal penalties.

The hedonist culture, which had replaced religion among the

educated, liberated classes, lumped intoxication and other rather different liberties together in a curiously indiscriminate way. They decided that everything they did not like was therefore wrong. Take the passage on 'Liberty and Gaiety in Private Life; the Need for a Reaction against the Fabian Tradition' in the conclusion to Anthony Crosland's *The Future of Socialism*[2] where he calls for a general 'change in cultural attitudes' which would make Britain 'a more colourful and civilised country to live in'.

The passage was written in 1956. Had it been written two decades later, might it have included a plea for a more relaxed view on drugs? I suspect so.

Sir Simon Jenkins, the highly respectable former Editor of *The Times*, feels no reluctance in identifying himself with the drug decriminalisation movement. Nor does Peter Lilley, a former Conservative Cabinet Minister, nor Bob Ainsworth, a former Labour Defence Secretary. Crosland, after all, voted with the unconventional moderns at the decisive 1970 Cabinet meeting, to give cannabis a special status and to reduce sharply the penalties for its possession.

Many who remember the 1950s will sympathise in general with Crosland's cry from the heart that

> We need not only higher exports and old-age pensions, but more open-air cafes, brighter and gayer streets at night, later closing-hours for public-houses, more repertory theatres, better and more hospitable hoteliers and restaurateurs, brighter and cleaner eating-houses, more riverside cafes ... .

It is only when we look carefully at it that we see that one part of this programme – the longer drinking hours – turn out not to have made life brighter and cleaner, but darker, more violent and more

---

[2] Constable and Robinson edition 2006, pp.402–3.

squalid. Crosland certainly did not know that this would happen or intend it. He thought that a change in the rules which suited him personally would also be good for the masses. It was not, because the masses are very unlike socialist intellectuals. But this is the case with many of the reforms pursued by him and his ally Roy Jenkins.

And so the plea to make Birmingham and Bradford more like Paris went on for line after line, with calls for murals in public places, new designs for telephone kiosks, statues on housing estates, better-designed women's clothes, streetlamps and furniture.

Pausing for breath, Crosland very significantly warned

> The enemy in all this will often be in unexpected guise; it is not only dark Satanic things and people that now bar the road to the new Jerusalem, but also, if not mainly, hygienic, respectable, virtuous things and people, lacking only in grace and gaiety.

Then comes a renewed attack on the licensing laws, together with an especially vigorous assault on the divorce laws (he was, while he wrote these words, coming to the end of his first bitter and unsatisfactory marriage, and plainly writes with personal feeling). He takes a swipe at Labour's 1956 National Executive for being sterner and more orthodox on this subject than the bench of bishops.

Crosland declares that most of the restrictions which he attacks (and which would be abolished during the 1964–70 Labour government) 'are intolerable, and should be highly offensive to socialists, in whose blood there should always run a trace of the anarchist and the libertarian, and not too much of the prig and the prude'. In a footnote, he complains that opposition to relaxed drink licensing laws is 'nauseating'. These attitudes certainly leave room for the acceptance of some drug taking, and for the generally more relaxed moral atmosphere that accompanied the rock and roll revolution. They also emphasise the conflict between Crosland's 'anarchist and libertarian' view and the 'priggish and prudish' or 'hygienic, respectable and virtuous' chapel attitude. This puritanical view of the world more or less completely disappeared from the Labour Party during the Blair revolution, so often wrongly described as a victory of 'Right' over 'Left'.

12

The left casts off its puritan garments

Proclaiming himself to be in the socialist tradition of William Morris, Crosland complains that Labour's Nonconformist and Fabian influences 'wear a bleaker and more forbidding air' than his part of the movement.[1] He then laughs at the Fabian Webbs, who spent their honeymoon 'investigating Trade Societies in Dublin' and returned from a later visit to the USSR to exult that 'there is no spooning in the Parks of Recreation and Rest'. He recognises that their austerity, their self-discipline and their insistence on 'immunity from physical weakness above all other virtues' served their purpose in another era.

> But now we surely need a different set of values ... Now the time has come for a reaction: for a greater emphasis on private life, on freedom and dissent, on culture, beauty, leisure, and even frivolity. Total abstinence and a good filing-system are not now the right signposts to the socialist Utopia; or at least, if they are, some of us will fall by the wayside.

---

[1] *The Future of Socialism*, pp.403–5.

should not continue to do so. They were not conscious revolutionaries, only a little spoiled by fame and money – two things capable of giving those who have them an inflated sense of their own importance, and a belief that they are or ought to be immune from the trivial rules which confine everyone else.

Their lives, and the activities which had made them rich and famous, were based on the happy uninterrupted pursuit of pleasure. The perpetual sunlight of the sixties springtime played in their hair. In the case of rock musicians, they also possessed an economic power and a cultural popularity that would make it very hard to keep them within the confines of the law. Not only did they contribute a great deal towards the nation's exports. They could afford the best lawyers.

A strange series of events was to align these rather trivial and silly people with a very serious campaign to change the world.

That campaign actually took the name 'SOMA' or 'The Soma Research Association' and we must all be indebted to the rigorous and drily humorous account of it.[3] This is provided by SOMA's brightest, sharpest and most effective member, a (then) young American called Stephen Abrams.

The campaign began in 1967. It exploded into prominence with an extraordinary full-page advertisement in *The Times* on 24 July of that year. *The Times* was in 1967 a newspaper whose reputation and influence was far greater than it is possible to imagine now.

The advertisement called for the decriminalisation of cannabis, and bore the signatures of all four members of the Beatles (each mentioning their recently awarded MBE decorations), the artists

---

[3] 'Soma, the Wootton Report and cannabis law reform in Britain during the 1960s and 1970s' which forms Chapter 4 in 'A cannabis reader: global issues and local experiences' published in Lisbon in 2008 by the European Monitoring Centre on Drugs and Drug Addiction.

John Piper and David Hockney, the Tory politician Jonathan Aitken, the Nobel prizewinner Francis Crick, the Labour MPs Brian Walden and Tom Driberg, the theatre director Peter Brook, the TV producer Tony Garnett, the novelist Graham Greene, the broadcaster David Dimbleby, the revolutionary student leader Tariq Ali, the journalist and TV presenter Brian Inglis, the theatre critic Kenneth Tynan, the publisher Tom Maschler, the psychiatrists Anthony Storr and R. D. Laing, the philosopher Alasdair MacIntyre, among several others.

One of the signatories, Michael Schofield, would shortly be a member of the very committee set up to examine the case he had advanced. Another, Michael Abdul Malik (also known as 'Michael X') would later be hanged for murder at the end of a sordid life. But he is the exception in a group which might well be said to be the Central Committee of the British Cultural Revolution.

I will return later to the details of the advertisement, and its message.

13

The mysterious spread of cannabis

But first it is important to know just why it was so timely and so important. Stephen Abrams explains that 1967 was a 'watershed year for cannabis'. He records the slow but definite growth in its importance and prevalence in this country, accelerating suddenly as the great Cultural Revolution picked up speed in 1967–8. As recently as 1951, there had been only 127 convictions for cannabis use or trafficking (the two crimes were then not treated as separate by the law) in the entire United Kingdom in the whole year, rising to 185 in 1959. According to Mr Abrams its use then rose till 'a plateau of about 600 convictions was reached in 1962, and not exceeded until 1966, when a figure of 1,119 was reached'. Something important was plainly changing by then, for in 1967 convictions doubled again to 2,393, with 600 lbs of the drug seized. These figures would certainly have seemed alarming to law enforcement officials of that time. But they were as nothing to what would soon happen.

'By 1997, cannabis seizures had increased 500-fold to more than

300,000 lbs impounded in a single year.[1] Comparisons of arrests and prosecutions were, as we shall see, not so easy to make. By 2009, 162,610 arrests were made for cannabis possession alone. A minority of these reached the courts, most (nearly 87,000) being dealt with by 'Cannabis Warnings', a procedure without legal force or significance In recent times about 1,200 cases of supplying cannabis, or of possessing it with intent to supply, have been dealt with by the courts each year.

Mr Abrams had written[2] that as many as 500 Oxford undergraduates – at a time when the universities were far smaller than they are now – were cannabis smokers, and that the University had not noticed. A popular Sunday newspaper, the *People* (as it then was), had picked up the article and used it as the basis for a page one story headlined 'Drug Sensation in Oxford'.[3]

This coincided with the publication – in the rival *News of the World* – of a two-part series drawing attention to the widespread use of drugs by rock stars, and the drug lyrics in their songs. 'Pop Stars and Drugs – facts that will rock you', it promised. It did not deliver very much – and a large part was devoted to the promotion of LSD in songs and on TV, by various middle-ranking musicians.

There were confessions, surprising then, commonplace now, of marijuana use by various performers. It quoted an 'authoritative' but unnamed survey saying that the number of heroin addicts could reach 11,000 by 1972. This does not look alarmist now. (The British National Treatment Agency for Substance Misuse estimated that there were 320,000 people in Britain dependent on heroin or crack cocaine in 2009–10). And it dwelt at length on a song called 'Night of

---

[1] The following figures are for England and Wales alone.
[2] In an article entitled 'The Oxford Scene and the Law' in *The Book of Grass*, edited by George Andrews and Simon Vinkenoog, Peter Owen, London 1967.
[3] 29 January 1967.

Fear', performed by The Move, which contained such lyrics as 'Your brain calls out for help that's never there', and 'these things you hear are too much for your mind'.

The following week, the newspaper made specific allegations against Mick Jagger. I shall not repeat the allegations here, ancient as they are. This provoked Jagger into a libel suit against the paper. It can truly be said to have set off the avalanche that eventually led to the Wootton Report and the Misuse of Drugs Act. What the Beatles would finish, two of the Rolling Stones began.

The *News of the World*, according to Steve Abrams, then approached the police asking them to act against the Rolling Stones.[4] Abrams says that a senior figure in the Metropolitan Police Drug Squad refused to act, saying privately that he was supposed to control cannabis, not stamp it out, and that if he arrested Mick Jagger 'every lad in the country would want to try some pot'.[5]

Abrams says the *News of the World* 'had more success with the local police in West Wittering, where Keith Richards lived'. The famous West Wittering raid, in a highly respectable seaside village in West Sussex, took place on the afternoon of Sunday 12 February but – puzzlingly, given the fame of those arrested – was not reported until a week later.

We will come in a moment to the Wittering arrests and their consequences. But what was happening to ordinary British subjects who were caught with cannabis in 1967? The risks were quite severe, and capable of destroying career hopes or severely restricting international travel. There was then, as noted, no distinction in law between

---

[4] The newspaper was closed down forever during the writing of this book (July 2011), partly thanks to allegations that it had made improper payments to police officers.
[5] This claim is made in 'The Wootton Retort, the Decriminalisation of Cannabis in Britain, by Stephen Abrams, published June 1997, revised August 1997.

possession and trafficking. Allowing one's premises to be used for drug crimes was an absolute offence. Steve Abrams records that one case in four (often of simple possession) ended in imprisonment. One in six first offenders was imprisoned. This was truly a 'war on drugs' or possibly even 'prohibition'. The question was whether the state and the justice system had the will to sustain it, or whether the cultural revolutionaries would overcome them. What remained of Puritan England was becoming alarmed at a social change it had not asked for and did not like.

But the unacknowledged legislators of the age, among them the pop music industry, were just as alarmed that serious application of the law would make the lives of many of them, and their friends, intolerable

There were many signs that the police and the courts still seemed to be determined to enforce the laws. The singer Donovan was the first major figure in the music industry to be affected. Donovan (his full name is Donovan Philips Leitch) had gained some fame with an act that looked and sounded quite like that of the American superstar Bob Dylan. He appeared in a national TV documentary on 19 January 1966.[6] A few months later he was arrested – in comical circumstances – in possession of cannabis. His fans and his friends in the music world were affronted by this application of the law.

The episode was more than slightly ridiculous. Having been arrested on 10 June 1966, in the middle of the night at his flat in Maida Vale, and then released on bail, Donovan came before Marylebone magistrates on 28 July. It was related that he had been in the company of an attractive young woman called Doreen, variously described as 'striking', 'blonde' and 'brunette' (a photograph shows

---

[6] 'A Boy called Donovan' on ITV – described as 'an entirely brainless programme' by Mary Crozier of *The Guardian*.

her clearly as blonde and certainly as striking). The striking Doreen had been unclothed when the police came hammering on Donovan's door, waving a search warrant. The presence of a naked or near-naked girl seems to have been almost essential at such arrests in this era. And why not? The sexual revolution was closely intertwined with the growth of the drug habit.

The prosecution declared that Donovan and his friend 'had been smoking cigarettes containing the drug cannabis (Indian Hemp)'. At this stage neither the law nor the newspapers could make up their minds what to call cannabis, or how to spell 'marijuana' (as they often termed it then), as it was so exotic and unfamiliar.

The singer was said to have tried to knock the warrant out of the officer's hand and to have become 'extremely violent' when cautioned. He was also said to have 'jumped naked on to the back of the police sergeant' who was trying to enter the room where Doreen was in bed.

Donovan's lawyer William Hemming intoned, in a rather confused plea: 'The very fact that these youths get embroiled in this way of life and this success so quickly, tends to lead them into what is sometimes called the Bohemian way of life, with all its concomitant temptations'. Bohemian it certainly was, or even 'Modern Unconventional'.

Donovan's friend 'Gipsy Dave' (otherwise known as David John Mills) had answered the door to the police 'wearing a shirt and nothing else'. He had then tried to slam the door and shouted 'Don! Don!' Donovan himself was said to have been swearing throughout the arrest, and to have told police in forceful terms not to go into the bedroom.

The prosecutor, stressing the singer's nudity, wanted the magistrates to be clear that this was not a respectable evening at home: 'He was completely naked. He was behaving most strangely and the air smelt greatly of cannabis smoking'.

against it are ridiculous, all foreshadow a thousand similar stories which at that time had yet to be told. In some ways they are like a provincial rehearsal, with amateurs, for the approaching drama at West Wittering, involving those giants of our age, Sir Michael Jagger and Lord Rees-Mogg.

It is also striking that, though the law was applied with moderate strictness, Donovan was not imprisoned, as he certainly could have been and as many were in those days. Authority was still trying to make up its mind what to do, and not – on this occasion –in the mood to make an example of a public figure for the general good. The real confrontation was yet to come.

It seems very likely that Stephen Abrams is right, and that the decisive battle of Wittering was brought on by the series in the *News of the World* (mentioned above) which was published a few months later, on 29 January 1967 and on 5 February 1967. This pair of articles had a great impact on the law and its enforcement – though probably not the one intended by their authors. They began portentously but correctly 'Ever since "beat" groups arrived on the scene to lay the foundations for Britain's pop culture – one of the most astonishing phenomena of the century – rumours have circulated that many young stars took drugs'.

The paper now claimed to have 'the facts' about these rumours. Perhaps thanks to the libel laws of England, it did not present very many of them. But it threatened more to come, and – in an episode oddly like the downfall of Oscar Wilde – the fulfilment of the threat led to a libel action which itself provoked a prosecution.

Until this unexpected crisis, and even after Donovan's fine, many in the rock music world had continued to believe they were immune from a law they regarded as futile and outmoded. For a brief and significant period, they were not molested, and their fame may have protected them. A few years later, especially under the direction of the London Drugs Squad chief Norman ('Nobby') Pilcher, the capital's police were to take an aggressive attitude towards the aristocrats of rock. Detective Sergeant Pilcher, like many others, did not realise which way the battle was really going. It is telling that Sergeant Pilcher (who is widely thought to have been mocked as 'Semolina Pilchard' in the Beatles song 'I am the Walrus') would end his career disgraced and in prison, while those he arrested went on to riches and honour. This outcome encapsulates the reversal which was about to take place, but which few, then and since, have properly understood or even acknowledged.

The atmosphere of 1967 fashionable London is well described by Barry Miles in *Many Years from Now*[7] his authorised biography of Paul McCartney. The police, in collaboration with parts of Fleet Street, were by then pursuing several musicians whom they suspected of taking illegal drugs. First there was the West Wittering raid in May 1967, which led to the trial and imprisonment of Keith Richards (one year) and Mick Jagger (three months). Soon afterwards their fellow Rolling Stone, the late Brian Jones, was arrested in his London flat for cannabis possession.

Richards and Jagger's management must have been appalled by the danger that their clients, at the peak of their fame and earning power, would no longer be able to tour in the USA, which generally refused entry to anyone convicted of drugs offences. They swiftly mobilised powerful legal representation, headed by the future Tory Cabinet Minister and Lord Chancellor, Michael Havers.

Jagger (though not Richards) also won the sympathy of the then William Rees-Mogg, editor of *The Times*. In a series of rather ridiculous events[8] Jagger and Richards were both exonerated, though

---

[7] *MYFN*, Secker and Warburg, London 1997.
[8] Described in detail in my *The Abolition of Liberty*, Atlantic Books, London 2004).

the sexual revolution and noting that Hindley and Brady had been exposed to pornography, and especially the works of the Marquis de Sade.

Snow suggests, much against his own radical inclinations, that there is a high price to be paid for this new sexual freedom. He makes several two-edged references to Wagner's 'Venusberg', the symbol of profane love in the opera 'Tannhäuser', which exalts the value of sexual love, and the virtues of oblivion.

Like Freddie Ayer, Snow – also a Godless socialist – was intelligent enough to see instinctively that the Brave New World might in fact be rather nasty when it arrived. But he was wrong to think that this revolution in behaviour was about sexual freedom alone. Precisely the same principle used by the sexual liberationists, that we should be able to do with our own bodies as we wish, is cited by the drug decriminalisation campaigners.

It is done with exactly the same object, the pursuit of pleasure. And it is not simply for any pleasure, but for a special new kind of pleasure separated from the effort, the commitment or the responsibility normally needed to attain it. Recreational sex, rendered 'safe' by contraceptives or easy abortion, breaks an ancient link between physical joy and fertility. It is not even pagan, since paganism is so deeply concerned with fertility, but something entirely new in human experience. Recreational drugs – as Allan Bloom points out – snap the ancient link between exceptional effort, courage and persistence, and the ecstatic, euphoric delights that these things can bring.

14

Jaggerism is invented

So what we might call Jaggerism – for Mick Jagger and his trademark lips are the universally understood symbol of this view – consists of asserting total sovereignty over our own bodies. It is John Stuart Mill with electric guitar accompaniment. This is the moral (or immoral) claim that lies behind (for example) campaigns for 'abortion rights', campaigns to belittle and dilute marriage, for the freedom to take dangerous drugs and for legalised prostitution. The attitude expressed by Keith Richards – 'We are not old men' – is also important. These beliefs, when first set forth, demanded some sort of conflict with parents and teachers, who were required to abandon their former authority and become passive childminders and facilitators. Once they had done this, which they did after several painful years of conflict, a sort of peace between the generations remained. But it is a peace of the defeated. Parents are no longer really parents, and teachers are no longer really teachers. If they acted as if they were, they would probably be prosecuted.

Essentially, it was a revolt against the religious and conscience-based moral system which had prevailed until shortly before, and was now disintegrating. One of the aims of this book is to point out that these alleged 'freedoms', particularly the liberty to take mind-altering drugs, are quite different in character from the older freedoms of that hedonism. He also notes, in words which contradict claims that cannabis users in Britain still face a severe and punitive regime:

> The situation in nineties Britain is that sentences such as those passed on Hoppy or Keith are virtually unknown unless large scale dealing is involved or the sentence is concurrent with another, more serious charge and has been used to make the other charge stick ... the members of Baroness Wootton's committee must be thanked for changes in the law that have kept thousands out of jail.[6]

This verdict was, interestingly, confirmed by John O'Connor, a former head of the Scotland Yard Flying Squad, in an article in the *Daily Express*.[7] He said,

> Cannabis has been a decriminalised drug for some time now. Although still illegal, somebody found by police in possession of a small amount for their own use will probably just get away with a caution these days. There is no record taken, no evidence that anything has occurred.

Things were to go a good deal further than that, less than ten years later, as we shall see.

This state of affairs is the result of clever and determined lobbying in 1967. Barry Miles describes how Stephen Abrams suggested a subtle and effective campaign to change the law as a whole. It is a fascinating example of successful, well-targeted political activism. An official committee on hallucinogenic drugs was – conveniently – already in being, chaired by Baroness Wootton.

Lady Wootton was unmistakably a radical liberal reformer. She

---

[6] MYFN, p.395.
[7] 'Why the Law Must Clamp Down on the HARD Drug Users', 15 February, 1994.

and her committee had been appointed, before Jim Callaghan's arrival at the Home Office, by the liberal Home Secretary Roy Jenkins. Its membership was, at the very least, open to persuasion. Abrams urged that the whole issue of 'soft drugs' and the law could be influenced by a timely intervention, in the form of an advertisement in *The Times*. He was confident that if Lady Wootton could concentrate her enquiry on cannabis alone, her committee would reach the same conclusions arrived at by the two earlier studies[8] which had said that cannabis was harmless.

Only a few years later, he could not have been so sure. But in 1967 the active ingredient of the drug, tetrahydrocannabinol (THC) had only just been isolated and almost nothing was known about its operation on the human body. Since then, an enormous scientific and political dispute, with major commercial implications, has erupted over the harmfulness or otherwise of this drug, a dispute which is still in its early stages and cannot be said to have reached any final conclusion. But there is now much to suggest that cannabis is by no means safe. The remaining questions concern the size of the risk. But at the time all this was hidden in the future. The argument would be a purely moral and cultural conflict.

Abrams then called Paul McCartney. The Beatle was 'horrified' to hear that Hopkins had been locked up. McCartney offered to put up most of the money for the planned advertisement and invited the group to his home the next day for further deliberations. Miles's description of this summit is hilarious. Abrams

> seemed to be in some trouble, pursing his lips, taking tiny little steps and muttering something about a chemical he had

---

[8] The Indian Hemp Commission of 1893–4 and New York Mayor Fiorello La Guardia's Commission of 1944.

Day in the Life' was banned from the BBC airwaves because of what the Corporation regarded as unmistakable mentions of drug taking. The Beatles at that time trod a careful line between respectability and raucousness. Much of their popularity depended on their sweeter songs, which were liked well outside the teen market. But their teen market would be lost if they became too suburban. It was a difficult course to steer. Identification with a mainstream campaign for the relaxation of the cannabis laws, arm in arm with Graham Greene, Francis Crick, David Hockney and Brian Walden, would detoxify them while keeping them on the side of the cultural revolution.

Now let us continue our journey back in time, to the intoxicated permanent springtime of the late 1960s. By this time, the country was in the later stages of the Harold Wilson government, the most socially and culturally revolutionary ministry in modern history. Wilson himself appeared to be respectable and uninspiring. Even his most radical lieutenants, Roy Jenkins and Anthony Crosland, spoke in reassuringly educated tones and dressed conventionally. Here were no enraged students hurling cobblestones at the riot police, as in De Gaulle's Paris. Here were sophisticated committee men, adept at changing history by the clever wording of a paragraph and the cunning timing of a Parliamentary division.

15

Bloomsbury takes over Britain via the airwaves

For the devotee of personal liberty in all things, this was the time of almost perfect luxury. His tastes and desires had been almost entirely decriminalised or freed from tiresome restrictions. There was sex and bad language on the TV, and even more of it in the cinema, in books and in radical magazines. But it was the TV that made most difference. The morals and ideas of Bloomsbury, once restricted to a small Bohemia in the capital, were now flowing into millions of homes through powerful transmitters, in the form of 'avant-garde' plays, propagandist drama and grittily radical documentaries.

Symbolic of the times was Joan Bakewell, presenter of the BBC programme 'Late Night Line-Up', a regular opportunity for revolutionary cultural propaganda. Nobody knew at the time what the private tastes and passions of this person were, though they might reasonably have guessed. We know in detail now, and they suggest that she could not really have been impartial on the issues of cultural and moral revolution, and nor could the organisation which employed her.

Mrs Bakewell, as she then was, was in those years engaged in a doubly adulterous affair with the playwright Harold Pinter (both of them were betraying spouses). There were drugs and rock and roll as well. In an interview with Jan Moir of the *Daily Mail* in March 2009, the woman who is now Baroness Bakewell of Stockport looked back fondly 'on those freewheeling times when the likes of Jimi Hendrix played live in the studio and everyone smoked joints. It got so bad that David Attenborough, then the BBC2 Controller of Programmes, complained about the Late Night Line-Up drug- taking'. According to Dame Joan:

> He said to the editor: 'Every time I walk past your studio, there is a distinct smell of weed. Can you possibly get it under control? Because people are going to notice and I don't want to have trouble.'
>
> He was wonderful. He protected us from our enemies and defended us. He would say: 'Watch your step.' He was great.

In other words, open law-breaking was taking place in the studios of the national broadcaster. That broadcaster was not some modish independent film-maker or underground magazine, but a national institution. It depended on law and authority for its very existence. Its studios were built, lighted and heated, its executives and performers paid with money raised through the licence fee.

The licence fee was and is a tax collected under the threat of prosecution and imprisonment. The BBC therefore has a very direct interest in the rule of law. But when a senior executive of the BBC became aware of this open breach of the laws against cannabis, he did not act to stop it, let alone call the police. He urged the lawbreakers to be more discreet about their lawbreaking. Baroness Bakewell of Stockport recalls this with a sort of fond joy, and no apparent conception that anyone might find it hypocritical.

And yet the radical left still cling to the idea that 1960s Britain was still in the hands of a reactionary, crabbed establishment determined to crush individual liberty.

By that time, they were already hopelessly out of date. Abortion was legal, divorce was about to be made easier than ending a car leasing agreement. Illegitimacy was rapidly losing its stigma. The punitive principle was being removed from the criminal justice system.[1]

A three-year spell at university, subsidised by the taxes of the poor, under the relaxed guidance of radical teachers and far from parental influence, was fast becoming an essential rite of passage for middle class young men and women, and a requirement for most desirable careers.

But the bill for these things, financial, moral and social, had yet to be presented. That would come 15 or 20 years later, and it would be blamed, when it came, entirely on Margaret Thatcher rather than on the cultural revolutionaries whose actions made much of Thatcherism's excess possible.

A largely conservative population had turned out to be surprisingly tolerant of these changes, though Mary Whitehouse's National Viewers' and Listeners' Association did briefly become a radical social conservative movement with the power to scare and annoy cultural revolutionaries such as Sir Hugh Carleton Greene, then director-general of the BBC.

Mrs Whitehouse was defeated and her campaign never widened into a serious political movement. This was partly because, to begin with, the full effects of the 1960s reforms were not felt. By the time they were felt, the legal changes that brought them about were

---

[1] For a fuller description and examination of these changes, see my 1999 book *The Abolition of Britain* and my 2004 companion volume *The Abolition of Liberty*.

half-forgotten, and few made the connection between the 1964–70 government and the changes it had wrought. This misunderstanding does not only affect the conservative-minded masses. To this day it is fashionable on the left to regard the Wilson government as a disappointment and a nullity.

Most of these changes were achieved by 'Private Member's Bills', a form of legislation in which the government whips provide indispensable time and signal informal backing from on high, while an individual MP takes credit or blame. Since such Bills never feature in general election manifestos and since support for them runs across party lines, there is not much the voters can do to complain or to punish those responsible.

But in one area it seemed as if the radical drive had gone a little too far. The giants of what was then called Pop Music (until shortly before that it had been Beat Music) had won a strange standing in the changing Britain of 1967. They were courted by businessmen and politicians, who wanted a share of their popularity and some part of the great heaps of money they were making. The four members of the Beatles had even been awarded decorations by the Queen – Members of the Order of the British Empire – once a recognition of a life of disciplined service to something staid but good. In an age when Mick Jagger is a Knight, this may not seem as alarming and strange as it did when it first happened. Several holders of the order, but nothing like enough of them to make a difference, sent their medals back to Buckingham Palace in protest. I do not think the Beatles often used the letters 'MBE' after their names, as they were entitled to do. But a moment was coming where they would do so with great effect.

These musicians, while enjoying their wealth and standing, also knew that they would lose their magic if they were too acceptable to the authorities, and above all to the parents of the teenage boys and girls who bought their records and went to their concerts. They were the priests and celebrants of the new religion of 'Do What Thou Wilt' that was fast displacing the shrivelled Christian faith. Their songs were its hymns. They spoke not just of sex and drugs (though they did have much to say about those things) but also of uncool teachers, rebellious daughters, the pointlessness of self-sacrifice, the futility of faith. Their concerts were its services. Their brushes with the law were, it now seems, its martyrdoms. Was this why so many of them lived faintly risky lives? Or is there (as I suspect) an organic connection between this kind of music and the morals and attitudes with which it is linked in the new trinity of Sex, Drugs and Rock and Roll?

There cannot be much doubt that music based on a loud and relentless drumbeat, as so much of it was and is, was designed to excite and arouse not only sexual feelings but that longing for some sort of action and confrontation that lurks in most young men. The androgynous appearance of many of the male singers seems also have aroused some strange frenzy in adolescent girls, who often screamed helplessly throughout Beatles concerts, entirely unable to hear the music they had supposedly come to listen to, while voiding their bladders on the seats and floors of halls and stadiums. It was noted that the screaming was always triggered when the Beatles began to sing in falsetto voices.

The lyrics of many of these songs, which slip almost unnoticed into the heads of those who listen to them, are also revolutionary. In some cases they contain messages which have sounded to many listeners like advertisements for drug taking. And those listeners have had their suspicions – or secret hopes – confirmed all too often when their heroes have been arrested and prosecuted for possession of illegal drugs.

This was the point at which the two rival societies of late 1960s Britain collided with a screech of tortured metal. Nobody then foresaw how huge the coming revolution would be, how the century of the self, foreshadowed by Freud, would now actually come to pass in the lives of the ordinary millions. They could not have known how sexual frankness would become normal in conversation and in broadcasting, how swearing would invade the language, how marriage would fall out of fashion, abortions number tens of thousands a year, fatherless families become commonplace. The sexual behaviour of the rock elite was unwelcome to most of the established middle class, but at this stage more or less a private matter. It concerned people whose lives were too odd and distant to touch the safe and orderly world of the British middle and working classes.

Drugs were different. They were more frightening. Their powers were mysterious and unknown. There was much talk of 'addiction', an apparently irresistible force which could take over a person's life against his will. These drugs had existed before, but had been confined to microscopic minorities of deadbeats and outsiders. Cocaine was barely known at all. The taking of heroin, already surrounded by laughable myths about its addictive power (though it is less habit-forming than tobacco) was even then treated more as a misfortune or disease than as a crime.

A fable has grown up that the system, under which a few registered addicts were prescribed their doses by a few doctors, was 'working' and would have contained the problem had it been maintained. This is a fiction. The system was already breaking down by then because unscrupulous and perhaps corrupt doctors were overprescribing to clients who then sold their surplus to 'friends', creating the beginnings of a market in this drug. What caused the huge increase in the taking of heroin was not the abolition of the old system, but the cultural change which made its considerable pleasures more acceptable to British people. It is astonishing how seldom anyone mentions that people inject heroin because they enjoy doing so and because they don't care about the consequences for themselves or others.

Something similar is true of the insidious weed, cannabis, the object of one of the slickest public relations campaigns ever waged. A frankly racialist government had been content to accept the limited use of this drug among 'coloured' seamen and jazz musicians, keeping it under control with prosecutions. But by 1964 it was clear that its use was spreading into the 'white' population. Protestant Britain, with its culture of self-restraint and sobriety, was giving way at its edges to a new society of self-indulgence.

At that time, politicians, as well as civil servants, senior policemen, judges and other authority figures, tended to be men in their late fifties or sixties. Where they were conservative they were inflexibly, thoughtlessly and often rather humourlessly conservative. They had little understanding of the new world that was coming into being around them, though they often disliked it. The days of 44-year-olds becoming prime ministers had yet to come. There was precious little sympathy between the generation still in power and the generation to follow, in most areas of politics or the law. Hardened and marked by war and depression, the elderly elite were not inclined to yield or to see much virtue in the world of OZ, Suzy Creamcheese and the Indica bookshop.

But the cultural elite, the heirs of Bloomsbury and of the 1930s left, were a different matter even if they too were in their fifties or sixties. And on this issue, they were about to show just how much power they could wield when they tried. They could recognise, instantly, that the battle over cannabis was a wider and larger conflict. The issue at stake was self-indulgence versus self-restraint. Supporters of each cause were prepared to accept disadvantages arising from their choice. But the apostles of self-indulgence were much better at politics than the supporters of self-restraint.

Something certainly changed the general attitude towards drugs which had been confined to insignificant fringe minorities for the first two thirds of the twentieth century. Though it is hard to believe it now, Britain had no significant drug problem at all before 1964. According to the Wootton Report,[2] United Kingdom convictions for cannabis possession stood at 4 (four) in the whole year of 1945, rising to 79 in 1950, 115 in 1955, 235 in 1960 and 626 in 1965. Then something happened. In 1966, the figure almost doubled to 1,119, and in 1967 doubled again to 2,393. We shall return later to more modern figures for this offence.

The report noted (in terms which could not possibly be used today) that

> ... in the early part of the period most seizures, (of cannibis) were of green plant tops, found in ships from Indian and African ports thought to be destined for petty traffickers in touch with coloured seamen and entertainers in London docks and clubs. By 1950 illicit traffic in cannabis had been observed in other parts of the country where there was a coloured population. In 1950, however, police raids on certain jazz clubs produced clear evidence that cannabis was being used by the indigenous population; by 1954 the tendency for the proportion of white to coloured offenders to increase was well marked, and in 1964 white persons constituted the majority of cannabis offenders for the first time.[3]

Figures were appended. In 1963, 296 offenders were 'white' and 367 were 'coloured'. By 1967, 1,737 were 'white' and 656 'coloured'. The report cited witnesses who attributed this not to 'immigrant influence' but to international movement of young people and new attitudes to 'experimentation' with mood-altering drugs. They

---

[2] Submitted to the Home Secretary 1 November 1968, published 3 January 1969.
[3] Wootton Report, paragraph 35.

explained the recent rise in convictions as a result of the formation of drug squads by many local police forces. These explanations may all have been partly correct, and it is possible that they are wholly correct. But it is also possible that they are not the whole truth. 'International movement' among young people was not especially great in 1964 or 1967, as the cost of travel was still relatively high. If there were 'new attitudes', then what had caused them to arise and replace the older attitudes? And what were they anyway? No doubt drugs squads, once formed, had to prove the need for their existence by arresting and prosecuting people for drug offences. But unless all their cases were fictitious, they do not seem to have met much difficulty in doing so. The explanation accepted by the committee is – as in almost all cases – the one most sympathetic to the cause of decriminalisation.

Those convicted were in those days briskly dealt with. Baroness Wootton of Abinger (whose appointment was in itself a sign of the answer the government wanted) would say later: 'The committee was very concerned that about 25 per cent of people charged with possession of cannabis go to prison and, indeed, 17 per cent of first offenders in this connection are sent to prison, which seems very strange'.[4]

This appears to have been an exaggeration, echoed in the text of the report itself which complains of a 'notably greater emphasis on fines and imprisonment for possession of cannabis than of other dangerous drugs'.[5] According to A. E. Bottoms, an academic criminologist writing in the 'Probation Journal' in 1969, the proportion of those convicted of cannabis possession who actually went to prison in that era was 21.2 per cent, compared with 24.8 per cent for heroin

---

[4] Interview with Bert Baker in the Communist daily the *Morning Star* 28 February 1969.
[5] In paragraph 80.

and morphine. The report gave the impression of greater severity by treating fines and imprisonment as a single category, when they plainly are not.

Well, why should a powerful committee (whose recommendations would be almost entirely adopted in a remarkably short space of time) be so concerned about this rather small matter?

16

Steve Abrams steps up to explain

To explain this we need to turn to the fascinating reminiscences of Steve Abrams, who necessarily stalks through these pages as a hugely significant actor, wrongly unrecognised by history. Mr Abrams has written an engagingly frank and revealing memoir of his involvement with the campaign to decriminalise cannabis, published by the European Monitoring Centre for Drugs and Drug Addiction (EMCDDA), and no belief in an official British 'War on Drugs' can survive a reading of his account. He ran the organisation named SOMA[1] which was to have an effect far greater than its tiny membership and brief life would suggest.

In the book this apparently magic drug is often mentioned (see above) and is central to the sort of society Huxley portrays.

Mr Abrams, who is quite smart enough to have understood the significance of his group's title at the time, explains the urgency of the campaign at that moment. He says that there had been a growing number of arrests of rock musicians starting with that

---

[1] p.92.

of Donovan in 1966, continuing with the prosecutions of Mick Jagger and Keith Richards in June 1967. He notes that the Beatles album 'Sergeant Pepper', released at what he calls 'the zenith of their creative power and influence' was 'saturated with references to cannabis and LSD'.

Abrams asserts that 'The Beatles, and Paul McCartney in particular, were advocates of LSD: a serious confrontation was brewing between fashionable alternative society and the establishment'.

Soma was looking for a way to put the topic of cannabis law reform on the political agenda, and also to influence the terms of the deliberations of the Wootton Committee. In particular, the aim was to persuade the subcommittee to report on cannabis alone, rather than in conjunction with LSD. This in turn was based on the assumption that there was a consensus of informed opinion that cannabis was less harmful than stimulants, sedatives and alcohol and confidence that the committee would discover this for themselves.

Abrams devised a brilliant and dramatic way of ensuring that this would happen. He organised the decisive full-page advertisement in *The Times*, whose message and timing were extraordinarily well-calculated, as we shall see. This advertisement was one of the single most effective pieces of propaganda in modern British history, as well as the greatest return on investment (it cost £1,800 at the time, equivalent to about £25,000 today).

Its effect was so profound that, as with most well-placed lobbying, most of those influenced by it do not even know that they have been influenced. They think that when they speak or write, or appear to think about this subject that they are expressing their own views. But they are not. They are expressing the view of a highly partisan minority, which has gained wide currency because it suits the spirit of the age. This is a rare occasion on which we can see how conventional wisdom is actually forged.

Abrams takes up the story again:

> The gesture which occurred to me was to take a page of *The Times* newspaper for a paid advertisement in support of the decriminalisation of cannabis. The advertisement would draw its force from a number of influential people who would put their names to it.[2]

When McCartney was told, he 'immediately realised that the advertisement would have the effect of switching the focus from LSD to cannabis and associating the Beatles with prominent authorities in a legitimate protest "within the system"'.

This is a vital detail: the switching of the focus from LSD, a drug which already had a dark and dangerous reputation, to cannabis, a drug which was far more easily (if falsely) portrayed as harmless.

All four Beatles agreed to sign the advertisement. All would mention their MBEs when doing so. According to Mr Abrams (and McCartney's biographer Barry Miles), Paul McCartney guaranteed to meet its cost. It was at this point that Keith Richards and Mick Jagger went to prison. *The Times*'s famous leading article, in a detail not often mentioned, condemned the punishment of Jagger, but did not take up the case of Richards. Abrams explains that this actually set back the campaign by some weeks:

> Rees-Mogg's leader made it clear that he considered amphetamine to be a 'soft' drug and Jagger's offence to be trivial. However, he seemed to regard cannabis as a dangerous narcotic and was not, therefore, prepared to question the sentence of a year in prison for Richards. *The Times* got cold feet and postponed the publication of the advertisement, which finally appeared on 24 July.

By this time, the campaign for cannabis legalisation had grown

---
[2] EMCDDA paper.

home, and achieving an extraordinary amount of favourable coverage for her committee and its views. Her own opinions on cannabis were highly eccentric for a person of her age at that time. Now they are the lazy mainstream view of the British establishment.

In an interview with the *Sunday Express* of 15 June 1969 she told Sally Hardcastle: 'I really do not believe that cannabis is any more dangerous than alcohol ... There is a great deal of difference between cannabis and hard drugs'. And she (though childless, and therefore not really qualified to say such a thing) confided that she 'would not be too worried' if a child of her own smoked marijuana 'provided it was in moderation'. But she swiftly added that she would prefer this fictional child not to do so, as it was against the law.

Barbara Wootton's greatest and most damaging achievement in a long life of radical campaigning would be to give official force to the baseless and scientifically absurd belief that cannabis is a 'soft' drug, not to be bracketed with 'hard' substances such as cocaine and heroin. Her committee, whose more influential members appear to have been prejudiced from the start, invented the system of classification which has ever since been part of the country's drug laws. How can it be so easily said that the report was prejudiced? Its bias leaps from almost every page.

This was evident to Jim Callaghan, who acted to forestall the report before it was published. He said on 23 January 1969 in the House of Commons, in answer to presumably planted questions on the report: 'To reduce the penalties for possession, sale or supply of cannabis would be bound to lead people to think that the government takes a less than serious view of the effects of drug taking'.

Callaghan anticipated many years of argument by the cannabis lobby that it was wrong to prohibit cannabis if alcohol and tobacco remained legal. Just because we have other 'social evils in this country at present', he argued, 'it would be sheer masochism to add to our evils by legislation to make it more easy for people to introduce another one'. He then declared, apparently decisively, 'It would be entirely contrary to Government policy to allow this impression to spread ... It is not the Government's intention to legislate to reduce existing penalties'.

In the light of what would happen later, it is interesting to note that a Conservative MP, Sir John Langford-Holt, supported the Labour Home Secretary. 'Where there is no knowledge or certainty of the physical or social effects of this drug,' he said, it would be a particularly inappropriate moment to take action in the direction recommended by the report'.

More interesting still was the contribution of Quintin Hogg, who said, 'Our judgement is almost exactly the same on this matter as that of the government'. In October 1973, as Lord Chancellor, Hogg would urge magistrates to go easy on cannabis possession and on small-scale dealing.

But both James Callaghan and Quintin Hogg would make even more clear and direct condemnations of the Wootton Report three days later, in a much fuller debate on the subject. Callaghan chose this moment to make his most explicit and direct attack on his predecessor, Roy Jenkins. He even used the expression 'permissive society', and seemed to be suggesting that the moral revolution, sponsored by Jenkins, was now at an end.

He said,

I think that it came as a surprise, if not a shock, to most people, when that notorious advertisement appeared in The Times in 1967, to find that there is a lobby in favour of legalising cannabis. The House should recognise that this lobby exists, and my reading of the Report is that the Wootton Sub-Committee report, which had been condemned by James Callaghan when it was published, and was at that time highly radical. The episode tells us something very interesting about the real nature of modern British government – mainly that socially conservative opinions have almost no influence on it, whatever party is in office. And that socially radical opinions occupy important and influential positions in the permanent establishment.

Here is what Jim Callaghan said, as his own Bill, which he had reluctantly piloted to the Commons, returned there under new management.

> I was worried by what the Home Secretary said about cannabis and I wonder whether he is right about people's attitudes when he gives approval to what the right hon. Member for Ashford (Mr. Deedes) said in the last Parliament—that we have not made our story credible about cannabis to the younger members of the public. I did not believe it when the right hon. Gentleman said it, and I do not believe it now. I advise the Home Secretary to think carefully about this.
>
> It is not my experience that the younger members of the public are in favour of smoking 'pot'. It is my experience that a small and very articulate group, who have managed to corner the Press and a great deal of the public media, express themselves in terms of a generation gap, and say that we do not understand, but the plain truth is, as far as I know it and as far as the most recent market research that I have seen has gone, that over 90 per cent of young people are in favour of stringent penalties against those who smoke 'pot'. I hope that the right hon. Gentleman will not use his office to give credence to a view which I believe is misplaced, so far as the overwhelming majority of young people are concerned.

I know the groups who say, 'Smoking cannabis has a lot to be said for it. Why should you interfere with our rights as individuals?' That is not the whole question, but I beg the right hon. Gentleman not to accept, without further tests, the view that young people as a whole take this view. I have no evidence for this indeed, my evidence is in the opposite sense.

So ended the last serious argument ever to be offered by a senior member of the British establishment, against the *de facto* legalisation of one of the most dangerous drugs known to man.

17

The long march – Wootton and after

In a way, Barbara Wootton's Committee has never ceased to sit, and the advertisement in *The Times* has never ceased to be published. Every few years since 1969, there have been inquiries and committees of apparently sober and respectable persons which have continued the work of Lady Wootton, Steve Abrams and the others. They have grown steadily more respectable, and have steadily been given more respect by the media and by the new establishment.[1] It is no longer necessary to spend thousands of pounds to get the case for cannabis prominently displayed in national newspapers. They do it all the time, unpaid, as do broadcasting organisations.

What did Wootton actually say, and why did she say it? I have described Barbara Wootton as the original leftist battleaxe, and this is indeed so. As the epigraph of this book, I quoted her words in her autobiography, 'Again and again I have had the satisfaction of seeing

---

[1] In 1992, on the twenty-fifth anniversary of the advertisement, a renewed call for legalisation was published, attracting far more signatures from a far wider milieu. The event was barely controversial.

the laughable idealism of one generation evolve into the accepted commonplace of the next'.

As with so much of the self-proclaimed progress of the twentieth century, her idealisms were a mixture of rational change and radical folly. It is tempting for the sympathetic radical to assume (for instance) that because she was right about female emancipation, she was right about everything else. It is tempting for the conservative to assume (for instance) that because she was wrong about marriage and crime and drugs, she was wrong about everything else. But of course both positions are folly. There is much to be admired about her single-mindedness, her huge capacity for work and her love of reason. She was obviously right about female emancipation and proved herself right by her own long and distinguished life. But it must also be said that when Roy Jenkins chose her to make a study of drugs, he did not do so because he expected a conservative report.

Equally, he knew that she was politically canny, and knew how to get her own way. So, the signatories of the great advertisement in *The Times* may have been disappointed in her. But should they have been?

Let us look at that advertisement. By the standards of today it is blatant and crudely designed, full of capital letters and wasted space. It is headed 'The law against marijuana is immoral in principle and unworkable in practice'. It opens with a quotation from Spinoza that begins 'all laws which can be violated without doing anyone any injury are laughed at' and ends 'He who tries to determine everything by law will foment crime rather than lessen it', which more or less continues to be the belief of the Simon Jenkins tendency today, and which might be quite sensible if it were not for the terrible, random power of cannabis to ruin the lives of those who use it, and of their families.

It makes five demands:

1   The government should permit and encourage research

into all aspects of cannabis use, including its medical applications.

2   Allowing the smoking of cannabis on private premises should no longer constitute an offence.

3   Cannabis should be taken off the Dangerous Drugs list and controlled rather than prohibited, by a new ad hoc instrument.

4   Possession of cannabis should either be legally permitted, or at most be considered a misdemeanour, punishable by a fine of not more than £10 for a first offence and not more than £25 for any subsequent offence.

5   All persons now imprisoned for possession of cannabis and for allowing cannabis to be smoked on private premises should have their sentences commuted.

It asserts that 'informed medical opinion supports the view that cannabis is the least harmful of pleasure-giving drugs and is, in particular, far less harmful than alcohol'. A number of doctors are paraded at the bottom right-hand corner of the page, testifying to the general harmlessness of cannabis. I wonder what they would say now, if asked the same question?

It adds in words since parroted in a thousand thoughtful leaders in the newspapers 'Cannabis is non-addictive, and prosecutions for disorderly behaviour under its influence are unknown'.

Since there is no known objective measure of addiction, a concept which on close examination turns out to be circular rather than scientific, no more than a matter of opinion and an excuse for weak will, the first assertion is not really very valuable. In an age where people are said, in all seriousness, to be 'addicted' to sex, the concept has surely lost all meaning.

what he called 'soft drugs' with 'becoming moderation'. They should take care over ascertaining the background.

It would be quite different when large parcels of cannabis were discovered, when a deterrent sentence would be justified. Interestingly, and illustrating the constant slide of the law in the same weak direction, this view was to be reversed in January 2012, when the Sentencing Council recommended that those in possession of as much as 13 lbs of cannabis should not face prison.

Hailsham advised the magistrates to distinguish between what he termed 'retail and wholesale trade', and between transactions among neighbours 'in the way of social intercourse' and transactions where money changed hands – expressing the curious belief that such neighbourly transactions did not involve money. He advised them 'Do not lose your heads as judges because the drug is new to your experience and has a sinister ring'. In the same speech he helped the transformation of the illegal drug user from culpable criminal to pitiable victim by insisting that 'the addict must be treated as a human being'.

He wound up his declaration of peace by saying 'Don't let your prejudice, if you have one, against the offence, lead you to deal unduly harshly with the offender'.

On the same day, the Home Secretary Robert Carr expressed satisfaction at increasing seizures of cannabis, which he saw as a sign of more effective law enforcement. He boasted, more vainly than he can have known, 'The United Kingdom has no substantial drug abuse and can claim modest success in fighting it'. Even as he spoke it was revealed that in the previous year – the first full year of operation of the 1971 Act – cannabis offences had risen by 37 per cent from 9,219 to 12,599.

Sir Edward Wayne's letter itself is surprisingly cautious about the moral problems involved in laws against drugs. It also accepts that cannabis has dangers. While asserting that those dangers may have been overstated in the past and the risk of 'progression to opiates' exaggerated, Sir Edward writes,

> We think that the adverse effects which the consumption of cannabis in even small amounts may produce in some people should not be dismissed as insignificant. We have no doubt that the wider use of cannabis should not be encouraged.

Alas, the rest of the report had precisely the effect of spreading the belief that its dangers are insignificant, and that its wider use is not a danger. Yet its authors knew what they were doing. After a long passage (unsurprisingly) about John Stuart Mill and the prevention of harm to others, they admit in a wonderfully Edwardian style that

> it has to be recognised that no hard and fast line can be drawn between actions that are purely self-regarding, and those that involve wider social consequences. If generally speaking, everyone is entitled to decide for himself what he will eat, drink or smoke, the fact remains that those who indulge in gross intemperance of almost any kind will nearly always become a burden to their families, the public authorities or both. Indeed, examples of actions which never in any circumstances involve social repercussions are by no means easy to find. Nor can it be said that any consistent principle dictates the occasions on which the law at present intervenes to protect the individual from himself.[5]

They go on to say that judgement must be made on the probable severity of damage the individual may do to himself, and the risk that in damaging himself he may injure others. Public attitudes are also

---

[5] Wootton Report, paragraph 15.

report. The effects of unmeasured drug doses on objectively unmeasurable mental health cannot be clearly quantified. They are likely to differ between individuals. It is now generally accepted that the effects are greater when cannabis is taken by the young, especially those in early adolescence – a group who were more or less cannabis-free in this country in 1969. This is surely an argument for caution, not for a major step towards liberalisation of the law?

Paragraph 30 performs the same trick of carefully mentioning a known criticism, as if to cover the authors against being accused of ignoring it, and then immediately dismissing it.

It recounts that:

> There have been reports, particularly from experienced observers in the Middle and Far East, which suggest that very heavy long-term consumption may produce a syndrome of increasing mental and physical deterioration to the point where the subject is tremulous, ailing and socially incompetent. This syndrome may be punctuated on occasions with outbursts of violent behaviour. It is fair to say, however, that no reliable observations of such a syndrome have been made in the Western World, and that from the Eastern reports available to us it is not possible to form a judgement on whether such behaviour is directly attributable to cannabis-taking.

Once again, while reports on the side of complacency are accepted without question, stern scepticism is directed against (equally vague and unquantifiable) accounts suggesting reasons for alarm. It is not that there is more evidence for alarm than there is for complacency. It is that the authors have already decided which vague accounts they wish to believe.

The report, which increasingly resembles an article in a left-liberal magazine, then moves on to describe the current levels of use of cannabis.

Government figures show a rapid increase in cannabis arrests (in the United Kingdom), from 51 in 1957 to 2,393 in 1967. The numbers had also begun to accelerate sharply after 1965, also around the time that what was then called 'Beat Music' had become a major cultural force. The total of arrests in 1966 had been 1,119; that in 1965 had been only 626. By 1972, they would reach 12,599. Yet these figures are as nothing to those which followed the full implementation of the Wootton Report. By 2009 there would be almost 163,000 cannabis arrests in England and Wales alone. And these would take place despite a general lack of interest by the police in troubling cannabis users at all.

These sections are purely factual. But paragraphs 39 to 43 are extraordinarily, almost simperingly sympathetic to the drug and its users. Wootton says:

> All our witnesses were agreed, that cannabis-smoking in the United Kingdom was a social rather than a solitary activity, casual and permissive like the taking of alcohol.

They do not stop to wonder why it had managed to interview nobody who dissented from this sympathetic and complacent view.

It continued:

> Friend introduced friend, the drug was readily enough available; if it did not suit the initiate, no one was the loser. The collective impression was that cannabis 'society' was predominantly young and without class barriers. It resented middle-aged society's judgement on alcohol and cannabis. It was not politically inclined and our witnesses saw no special significance in the popularity of cannabis among members of radical movements.

That was unobservant of them. However, the public relations presentation continues:

> Some witnesses thought it was possible to distinguish particular social groups within cannabis 'society' and mentioned staff and students in universities and art schools, jazz and pop musicians and entertainers, film makers and artists, And others engaged in mass media or publicity.[9]

Paragraph 41 asserts:

> The 'professional' group, for example was described to us as fundamentally law-abiding; discriminating in the use of cannabis for introspection and elation as well as for social relaxation; 'involved in life', often to the point of social protest; not much interested in experiments with L.S.D.; generally disinclined to take amphetamines or alcohol (which was regarded as much more damaging than cannabis); and tending to stop the use of cannabis on marriage, or when the risk of prosecution was felt to be inimical to career prospects.
>
> The 'unskilled' group was said to be similarly industrious and law-abiding and to see nothing wrong or harmful in its use of cannabis.

Following the long and admiring description of these paragons, paragraph 42 does at least mention

> young people who had failed to adjust to university life or professional training or regular work, or who had 'dropped out'; actively discontented and rebellious teenagers, looking for 'kicks', who were prepared to take any drug offered to them: their weaker

---
[9] Paragraph 40.

associates who took cannabis to avoid rejection by the group; and a few who were severely unstable and sought escape from their problems in a multiple drug use that included cannabis.

But it quickly adds that 'We judged that they, the witnesses interviewed, considered the responsible law-abiding users to be the majority'.[10]

I have quoted these passages because they seem to me to have no place in a government report on the safety or otherwise of an illegal drug. They offer subjective social and cultural arguments, not scientific ones. Also, their tone is undoubtedly sympathetic to cannabis users. Later, in paragraph 45, an almost lyrical description is given of the drug's effects on its consumers: 'relaxing and calming', 'beneficial to young patients during depression'. It was even said to 'have helped ex-addicts to abstain from heroin'. While noting that some contested this, and warned that it created anxiety and passivity, it swiftly moves on to 'euphoria, tolerance of the environment, and at a more intellectual level heightened awareness of self'.

One of the medical witnesses mentions 'a few cases of acute psychosis', quickly adding that he 'did not feel completely satisfied that cannabis had been the cause'.

The same witness mentioned 'severe disturbance in a sample of chronic users' but 'as this group was self-selected this information seemed to be of doubtful relevance to the generality of experience of cannabis-taking'. As in the early sections, the report is quick to write off any suggestions of danger, and equally quick to welcome and emphasise any indications that the drug is beneficial and harmless.

The report goes on to quote approvingly a report from Oakland, California, in which young cannabis users were 'firm in their

---

[10] Paragraph 43.

conviction, based on their own experience, that the use of such drugs as marihuana resulted in harmless pleasure and increasing conviviality, did not lead to violence, madness or addiction'. It was also (of course) less harmful than alcohol and 'could be regulated'.

The same relentless drumbeat of propaganda which we hear daily today is to be found here, in what is perhaps its original version. Alcohol is bad. So why be so hard on cannabis? Once again, the reader wonders what these arguments are doing in a report of this kind. Paragraph 61: 'It is impossible to make out a firm case against cannabis as being potentially a greater personal or social danger than alcohol'. Amusingly for a reader in the twenty-first century, paragraph 64 mocks past attempts to stamp out tobacco smoking by law, saying 'Tobacco was once the subject of extreme judgements' it then lists several seventeenth-century attempts to stamp out its use by law, including such penalties as nose-slitting, torture and decapitation. Little did they know how effective the law would eventually be against this habit, disproving once and for all the belief that legal restriction of drugs will always fail. By paragraph 70, the authors are cautiously accepting that, yes, cannabis is a 'dangerous drug' but as usual, swiftly qualifying their judgement. 'In terms of physical harmfulness, cannabis is very much less dangerous than the opiates, amphetamines and barbiturates, and also less dangerous than alcohol'.

There is, at paragraph 63, one extremely sensible point: 'To make a comparative evaluation between cannabis and other drugs is to venture on highly subjective territory. The history of the assessments that have been given to different drugs is a warning against any dogmatic judgement'.

It is a pity that the report itself chose to be subjective about its assessment of cannabis as (for instance) 'less dangerous than alcohol'. By what objective measure could this possibly be said?

And that is, more or less, that. The two elderly reports are reproduced.[11] There are pages of subjective and opinionated waffle in which cannabis smokers are treated highly sympathetically. Plenty of caveats and escape clauses are inserted in case cannabis is later shown to be more certainly dangerous than the authors believe, though they presumably knew that proving such a danger would always remain difficult. And then the recommendations follow.

Their tone is set in paragraph 67 in words which were then, and still remain, highly debatable: 'The evidence before us shows: that an increasing number of people, mainly young, in all classes of society, are experimenting with this drug'.

This use of the word 'experiment' has become almost universal in such discussions. In what way are its users 'experimenting'? Are they taking careful notes, comparing the effect of measured doses on people of different physiology or age? No, they are taking an illegal drug for pleasure. The word dignifies a squalid action with an undeserved glow of scientific endeavour. Its use in this argument is always a sign of bias, conscious or unconscious, in favour of drug use.

Wootton continues: 'There is no evidence that this activity is causing violent crime or aggression, anti-social behaviour, or is producing in otherwise normal people conditions of dependence or psychosis, requiring medical treatment'.

If anyone had blamed cannabis at that time for violent crime, I am not aware of it.[12] This is acquittal of a charge not levelled. But in fact, by the rather low standards of evidence in this document, there is evidence of aggression and psychosis in some of the passages that I have quoted. The assertion of the report conflicts with its own text.

---

[11] Indian Hemp and La Guardia, p.145.
[12] Though some of the accounts I reproduce above do suggest a possible link.

to create a de facto decriminalisation, one which the government need not acknowledge, and one which can be continued almost indefinitely into the future.

As we have seen, the Cabinet would move strongly in the direction called for by the Committee. But it did so behind a screen of apparently conservative noise and shouting, which succeeded in giving the opposite impression. It was the report's publication which produced James Callaghan's roll of thunder in the House of Commons against the tide of permissiveness[14] – an outburst which may well have been genuine. It also resulted in his clear declaration (in reply to Parliamentary questions a few days earlier) that 'it is not the Government's intention to legislate to reduce existing penalties'. *The Times* headline on this account is straightforward and accurate: 'Cannabis penalties not to be reduced'. The press of the time also suggested open conflict between the Home Secretary and the Advisory Committee on Drug Dependence.

On 5 February Baroness Wootton and Sir Edward Wayne, chairman of the main official committee on drugs, wrote to *The Times* to say that it had been 'offensive' of Mr Callaghan to suggest that the Wootton sub-committee were 'over-influenced' by the lobby in favour of legalising cannabis. This is very strong language indeed, on both sides, in a Whitehall battle. The letter states quite correctly that of course the report does not advocate legalisation. This has, ever since, been one of the most effective positions of the pro-drug lobby. By portraying themselves as more responsible than the wild legalisers, they manage to appear moderate and reasonable, and open to compromise. A poorly informed public is reassured that no major changes are happening. And the intended aim – the relaxation of the law to the point of nullity – is achieved.

---

[14] p.131–2.

By late February, the *Sunday Times* was reporting that 'Next Friday the 20 angry members of the ... Advisory Committee ... meet to decide how to react to the savage Parliamentary mauling they have received at the hands of Mr James Callaghan'.[15]

In an article lacking much impartiality, Alexander Mitchell wrote that Mr Callaghan 'made the incredible statement that the committee, comprising distinguished doctors and psychologists, had been "over-influenced by the pot lobby"'. I am not sure why this statement is 'incredible'. It would seem to be a reasonable response to the tone of the report.

But Mr Mitchell continued,

> This was the final emasculating blow to fall on the committee, which had already come under censure from the Press, the public and even agencies of the United Nations. Possibly no committee set up by the government of the day has seen its work devastated so brusquely.

There was repeated talk of members of the committee resigning in protest at their treatment. John Stevenson wrote in the *Daily Sketch* that 'the resignation of the entire committee will be considered at a meeting next Friday'.[16] The same report said that the Home Secretary had 'ordered the drafting of a White Paper outlining a tougher anti-drugs policy without consulting the advisory committee'. It continued: 'His move is regarded as the second snub for the team which he attacked last month over its cannabis report'.

As I describe in earlier chapters, the battle ended with James Callaghan conceding a great deal of ground. Cannabis was given a

---

[15] 23 February 1969.
[16] 24 February 1969.

When the penalties for offences are reduced as those for cannabis possession have been, the state is signalling to the police to bother less with the crime concerned. They duly do so, and that offence becomes more widespread. Reversing this process requires a more-or-less revolutionary reversal of policy.

And this is why all schemes to weaken the drugs laws nowadays win the noisy approval of almost all senior police officers. They have become one of the strongest lobbies for drug liberalisation in the country. It is also the case that a growing number of senior and chief officers no longer come from the traditionally morally conservative parts of society which once supplied most policemen. They are recruited from the post-1960s generation of university graduates which views cannabis-smoking as a civil liberty and a victimless crime.

Mr O'Connor, despite his background in the rougher and least graduate-infested areas of policing, appears to have been thoroughly bamboozled by the incessant propaganda of the cannabis lobby. 'This type of user', he wrote of cannabis victims, 'is hardly a big threat to society, and taking this new puritanical approach, the police will not only be wasting a lot of time, but also losing hard-won public credibility'.

'They aren't the kind to stick a knife in your back and take your wallet, or organise a break-in and distribution of the stolen goods', he wrote. It is hard to say whether this is true, but it is not the point in any case. The police act against all kinds of people who do not fall into this narrow category of crime. Many of those they zealously pursue for offences against political correctness certainly do not knife anyone in the back or steal any wallets.

Mr O'Connor also does not explain how 'credibility' should or could be gained by failing to enforce the law. On the same scale, armies would gain credibility by not fighting battles, authors by not writing books and firemen by leaving buildings to burn down.

18

Widdecombe unfair

I must begin this chapter with a tribute to my sometime colleague on the *Mail on Sunday*, Jonathan Oliver. Mr Oliver, by doing his job diligently and enthusiastically, helped to clarify once and for all that the Conservative Party was on the side of liberalising the drug laws. The events which he recorded took place in Bournemouth in October 2000, when the Tory Party was still seeking a response to the extraordinary hypnotic power of Anthony Blair. Many of its members and supporters still had strong socially and morally conservative instincts – not least because of the Blair government's keen embrace of political correctness. The then party leader, William Hague, seemed ready to encourage such instincts, to rally his beaten party and perhaps – if successful – to provide it with a distinct response to Blairism. At that time his Shadow Home Secretary, the extraordinary figure of Ann Widdecombe, was widely recognised and admired by many for her uncompromising and unembarrassed readiness to be unfashionable.

But as well as being admired by some, she was despised by others. The Tory Party was at the time said to be divided between 'Mods', social liberals, supporters of the former Defence Secretary Michael Portillo, and 'Rockers', epitomised by Miss Widdecombe. This was a half-joking reference to youth gangs of the mid-1960s, motorcycle-riding, greasy haired, leather-jacketed rockers, and scooter-riding, fashionable mods, who used to battle with each other in beach-front resorts on summer afternoons.

Mr Portillo fought hard to make sure the 'Mods' were victorious. By doing so, he made the way straight for David Cameron, who would eventually stroll effortlessly on to the summit which Mr Portillo had striven so hard – yet so unsuccessfully – to reach, using the ropes and footholds which Mr Portillo had left for him.

Many thought they could detect Michael Portillo's hand in the fate which befell Miss Widdecombe, and which destroyed social conservatism in the Tory Party for the foreseeable future. But of course it is impossible to prove such things, and I shall not try.

Miss Widdecombe, almost as broad as she was tall, her hair in those days unbleached and uncompromisingly sculpted into a black pudding bowl, stumped on the stage, and strode about, declaiming in her unlovable, grating voice a fierce speech she had learned by heart, proposing a fixed penalty for cannabis possession. In truth it was not that radical, involving only a fine of £100 – which fell well on the liberal side of the Wootton Report's 1969 call for no further imprisonment of cannabis users. It did, however, mean a criminal record for those fined. And the pro-cannabis lobby was already hoping for an arrangement which would mean no fine and no criminal record – as we shall see in the next chapter.

She made the speech. It attracted much coverage, plenty of it favourable, and for many people it would probably have been the most memorable event of a rather bumpy conference, during which Mr Hague was spitefully dismissed as a 'dead parrot' by the *Sun* newspaper,[1] then a slavish supporter of the Blair government. But the Tory 'Mods' had other plans.

---

[1] And portrayed as such on Page 1.

Jonathan Oliver here takes up the story, a fascinating account of real political brutality:

It was the small hours of Thursday morning and the bar of the Swallow Highcliff hotel was heaving ...

Some noisily voiced their views on the leader's upcoming speech which would bring the Bournemouth conference to a close while others sealed plans to travel home together later. But for one or two the week's business was far from over.

A senior party aide had a message to impart. Placing his glass of champagne on the bar, he leaned forward and quietly explained how half the Shadow Cabinet were furious at the controversial plan by Shadow Home Secretary Ann Widdecombe to target cannabis smokers.

'Ask some of them whether they smoked dope when they were younger. I promise you will receive some fascinating responses,' he murmured before disappearing into the crowd.

Later that morning, the *Mail on Sunday*, acting on his suggestion, set about contacting William Hague's frontbench team. The result was astonishing. Over the next 36 hours there followed the most extraordinary series of revelations, which could tear the Tory Party apart and have major implications for Britain's drugs policies.

The aide, as Jonathan Oliver soon discovered, had been telling the truth. Shadow Foreign Secretary Francis Maude told the *Mail on Sunday* that he had taken the drug: 'I suspect, like many people of my generation, it was quite hard to go through Cambridge University in the Seventies without doing it a few times. It was an extremely long time ago'.

Next, the Shadow Transport Minister Bernard Jenkin told his story: 'I really only used cannabis a couple of times', he said. 'I would not want to give the impression I was doing it all the time. It was in my early 20s. It was miles before politics'.

The story continued:

> Within hours, other members of the Shadow Cabinet were opening up about their drug experiences. They denied colluding, but as they talked more freely to *The Mail on Sunday* it became obvious that this was more than just a chance to get a bit of youthful excess out in the open. Personal reputations and political career prospects were being laid on the line as well as possible opprobrium from the party faithful, friends and even family.

But the senior Tories' animosity towards Miss Widdecombe was enough to make them own up to having broken the law. The group was determined to soften Conservative social policy, in order to win support among younger voters; by speaking to the press, they could effectively mock Miss Widdecombe as out of touch. As Oliver wrote, this was 'a challenge by a third of the Shadow Cabinet to Mr Hague, forcing him to choose between them or Widdecombe who they now want removed from the law and order job'.

Archie Norman, the Tory spokesman on the environment, transport and the regions, said he took cannabis while a student at Cambridge, Harvard and the University of Minnesota in the United States. He added.

> I don't regret having done it. It didn't do much for me. I turned to drink instead. I was just a normal student like anyone else. It was fairly commonplace. It doesn't worry me at all what people think. I think you expect human beings to explore and experiment. If you don't you haven't been young.

'I didn't want to live my life without discovering what it was like,' said the Shadow Culture Secretary Peter Ainsworth, describing how he tried cannabis and the chemical 'upper' amyl nitrate at Oxford University parties in the seventies. Somewhat inconsistently, he added, 'The fact is that young people are going to experiment. But it is potentially dangerous ... I would advise everybody to steer well clear'.

Social Security spokesman David Willetts, 44, admitted trying marijuana; Lord Strathclyde, party leader in the Upper House, admitted to trying cannabis 20 years previously. Oliver Letwin said he had done so by accident at Cambridge.

Of the 14 other Shadow Cabinet members, nine denied they had tried drugs, two were unavailable and three – Shadow Chancellor Michael Portillo, Shadow Agriculture Secretary Tim Yeo and Ulster spokesman Andrew Mackay – refused to answer.

The openness displayed by such senior political figures on their drug-taking pasts will shock some Tories. Traditionally they have boasted of being the party of law and order but these 'confessions' indicate the way social issues dominate today. Hague seems to have brought most of the party together in opposing the euro for the immediate future. Now it is issues of behaviour and morality that are threatening to tear it apart.

Widdecombe's speech had been part of a struggle for coverage and supremacy, waged against the then Shadow Chancellor (and leader of the 'Mods'), Michael Portillo. Portillo supporters claimed she had acted – and had briefed journalists – without clearing her speech with colleagues.

Certainly she did not seem to have cleared it with the police, by then (as discussed) often the strongest supporters of weakening the drug laws. Soon after she spoke, Peter Williams, secretary of the Police Superintendents' Association, said, 'Our priority is not to punish people for possession but to divert them from drugs'.

19

Dame Ruth Runciman and the liberal establishment

Earlier the same year, another prominent woman in British Politics, Dame Ruth Runciman, had received the warm support of the establishment – if not of all the media – for advocating yet more defeatism in drugs policy.

Dame Ruth chaired a grandiosely named 'Independent Inquiry into the Misuse of Drugs Act 1971'. Who is she? Who were her fellow-inquirers? How did the committee come to be set up?

Dame Ruth is a very interesting person. She prefers not to use her title (through her second husband's hereditary Viscountcy), as she is a DBE in her own right. She described herself in an *Observer* interview[1] as 'the ultimate do-gooder'. In this, she was and is a worthy successor to Barbara Wootton, who fulfilled a similar role in an earlier Britain.

She has been part of the British liberal drugs establishment since the days of Roy Jenkins, who appointed her to the Advisory

---

[1] 14 January 2001.

obviously too close to a general election for any government to act on its recommendations.

Dame Ruth later revealed a conscious and deliberate link between her report and Brian Paddick's experiment of weakening the law in Brixton.[4] Her letter to *The Times*, published on 23 July 2001, with the general election safely out of the way, offered a rare glimpse of the smoothly oiled workings of the liberal establishment, normally well hidden:

> The pilot scheme being run by the commander of Lambeth Police in Brixton reflects the inquiry's recommendations precisely. What is urgently needed is reform, which would bring the harm done by cannabis and the harm done by the law into better balance, close the gap between what the law says and does and ensure that what applies in Brixton applies equally everywhere.

This letter makes the connection between her report and the Brixton experiment quite clear. Both were conscious steps in the same direction, understood by each other if not actually planned together.

She was also unable to conceal her delight at the Tory Party's political destruction of Ann Widdecombe, telling an admiring Victor Sebestyen in the *Evening Standard*[5] that she viewed Miss Widdecombe's defeat as a gift to the radical cause:

> Lady Runciman is profoundly grateful to the Shadow Home Secretary (Ann Widdecombe) for bringing the issue of drugs to the nation's attention. The fall-out from Widdecombe's conference speech last week may have done her no good in the Conservative

---

[4] p.196.
[5] 20 October 2000.

Party. But it has done the rest of us a favour. 'I never look a gift-horse in the mouth, wherever the gift comes from,' she says.

Mr Sebestyen, like most of the British media, was quite happy to let his sympathy show. He wrote that Dame Ruth's report was 'warmly welcomed at the time by almost everyone who knew anything about the drugs problem'. Tellingly, and echoing some words in the report itself, she told him that:

> The so-called war against crime is unwinnable. You cannot eradicate demand. It is an unachievable goal. You can have sensible and rational policies to contain the problems and the knock-on effects on health and the family. That was our aim.

But of course those who wish to use the criminal law to deter and interdict demand do not believe that it can be *eradicated*. They believe it can be diminished and deterred, and that it should be, because the drugs involved do so much damage to individuals to their families and to society as a whole. Like so many of her fellow campaigners, Dame Ruth seems to have ignored the idea that there might be a *moral* objection to taking mind-altering drugs. By stating an impossible goal, and saying that because it is impossible it should not even be sought, Dame Ruth simply avoids any discussion about why laws are worth enforcing at all, and why a law against drug possession might be beneficial.

By stating that existing penalties are not working, without emphasising that those penalties are in fact not strongly or consistently enforced, her report also gave the impression that it was strong enforcement that had failed. This closed any discussion of whether a tightening of the law – a policy rarely if ever discussed – might have produced a different result.

The committee, while it lacked any conservative voice, also

contained some notable supporters of loosening the law – Sir Simon Jenkins and Professor David Nutt among them. It is hard to see in what way the inquiry was 'Independent'. On the contrary, it was, from its inception, the voice of the establishment, which had long ago made up its mind that cannabis was harmless and not worth fighting.

Another matter that arises here is the question of race. Ever since the Brixton disorders and the Scarman Report[6] there had been a worrying tendency among some police forces to accept the idea that criminality, especially involving drugs, was in some way part of the culture of such areas. In fact the law-abiding majority in such districts was just as keen on law enforcement as it was anywhere else. The idea that drug criminality is more acceptable in a racially sensitive area can itself be seen to be, after a moment's consideration, a racialist idea. This concept would actually be accepted and endorsed in the Macpherson report, which specifically called for an end to 'colour-blind policing',[7] implying different sorts of policing in areas with high concentrations of ethnic minorities. It was certainly far too easy for criminals in such areas to cry 'racism' when the law was impartially applied to them.

The softening of the police presence in such areas was a far easier road for senior officers than continuing hard enforcement of the law, and then being blamed by liberal judges and politicians for any disorder that followed. Such blame is the logic of the Scarman Report, which actually admits that the police actions which triggered the Brixton disorders were entirely legitimate and justified, but then dignifies a criminal outbreak with the attributes of protest and sidles delicately away from evidence (which it acknowledges exists) that the criminality may have been organised.

---

[6] See my *Abolition of Liberty*.
[7] See my *Abolition of Liberty*.

It is almost certain that fear of another Brixton, reinforced by the post-Macpherson fear of being criticised for 'institutional racism' plays a large part in the current police enthusiasm for *de facto* decriminalisation of cannabis. Rigorously enforcing even the 1971 Misuse of Drugs Act, before it was modified by ACPO (Association of Chief Police Officers of England and Wales), would certainly have been met with anger among drug-abusing lawbreakers. And such anger would have been portrayed as 'anti-racist' protest – and as evidence of police 'racism' by liberal media and by the legal and political establishment. Who can blame the police for seeing which way the wind was blowing?

Dame Ruth continues with a classic statement of the appeaser's view of the cannabis problem – that prosecution of the drug abuser is worse than the effects of the drug itself. Now, as in all use of the criminal law, there is a question of how willing society is to defend itself against particular threats. Of course it is unpleasant and often painful to arrest and imprison people, and burden them with criminal records. But this is done, and always has been done, to deter others from committing the crime involved. The drug appeasers almost never examine the nature of that crime.

Dame Ruth had no doubt that she was on the winning side. She concluded,

> I do feel confident change will come. We came to the very clear conclusion, after the most expert of evidence, and much international research, that the current cannabis laws cause more harm than they prevent. The adverse consequences on life, for large numbers of young people, to have a criminal record – people who are in all other ways law-abiding – is absolutely disproportionate, and unnecessarily blighting.

She had good reason to be confident. Was there, at any stage, any serious doubt that her committee would produce any other report than the one that they did produce? Was there any doubt that the establishment, which willed the inquiry, would welcome its conclusions? Did they know, long before, what those conclusions would be?

Here is one clue. Dame Ruth told an ACPO conference on drugs in Preston on 1 May 1992, five years before her inquiry was set up: 'People are more likely to be cautioned than fined for minor drug offences, such as possession of cannabis'.[8] But she called for a national policy that got rid of the differences in cautioning rates between local forces. Put simply, she had already formed this opinion long before she was picked for the job, whoever picked her; and the authorities and the police were aware of it.

So the 'Independent' Inquiry's 'independent' chairwoman was from the start moving in one direction. And that direction clearly informed everything that followed. There seems to have been no dissenting voice on the committee. At the very beginning of its 'Overview', the report baldly states its defeatist view:

> In the course of our Inquiry it has become inescapably clear to us that the eradication of drug use is not achievable and is not therefore either a realistic or a sensible goal of public policy. The main aim of the law must be to control and limit the demand for and the supply of illicit drugs in order to minimise the serious individual and social harms caused by their use. At the same time, the law must enable the United Kingdom to fulfil its international obligations.

It is equally true that the eradication of burglary, murder, insurance fraud, drunken driving, speeding, cigarette smoking and many other undesirable acts is not achievable. Yet the law, in various forms, is still used in a determined and systematic way to reduce all these things

---

[8] *The Independent*, 2 May 1992.

to the lowest level possible. To abandon the struggle against a crime because it is ineradicable would be to abandon the struggle against all crime. And once again, the strange logic of the Misuse of Drugs Act is made plain. If the law is aimed at controlling and limiting the *demand* for illicit drugs, then how can it do so if users are not themselves subject to legal sanction?

Perhaps the most interesting point is that about international obligations. One of the reasons why legalisers seldom if ever admit to favouring actual legalisation is that they know that governments are forbidden, by treaty, to make these drugs fully, formally legal. On the other hand, they are free to reduce penalties to the point where they are no longer significant, and to fail to enforce the law. That is why they adopt such expressions as 'decriminalisation' and 'regulation', and will often protest angrily if they are accused of favouring legalisation. They also know that uninformed members of the public will be reassured by such protestations. Meanwhile, huge and significant changes, amounting to legalisation in all but name, can be made – if subtly applied – to fall just inside the rules set by international law. But subtlety is essential.

That is why paragraph 12 is in many ways the most important part of the whole Runciman report. It explains that the United Kingdom is bound by three international conventions, and that although there is

> a widespread belief that these obligations rule out the possibility of changes to the law ... *the conventions allow more room for manoeuvre than is generally understood* (my italics). All our recommendations fall within the requirements of this country's international commitments.

Soon after comes clear evidence that Sir Simon Jenkins is one of the members of this body. For it contains the standard false premise of the drug liberalisers' argument, Sir Simon's favourite point:

We have found that the United Kingdom has *a more severe regime of control over possession offences than most of the other European countries which we have studied* (my italics). Although direct comparisons are difficult because of incompatibilities as well as deficiencies in both the quality and quantity of the data, we have seen no evidence which would warrant the conclusion that the United Kingdom has benefited from the *more punitive provisions of its law on possession* (my italics)'.

This is a simple failure to distinguish appearance from reality. In fact, even if Sir Simon genuinely had not noticed the truth, Ruth Runciman knew perfectly well that the English drug law was not a 'severe regime' and that its 'punitive provisions' were a dead letter. As she stated in a BBC forum in October 2001:

Well, it's worth saying that of the offences against the Misuse of Drugs Act – these are very round figures as I don't have them to hand – of the 120,000 offences against the Misuse of Drugs Act every year, 90 per cent of those which are dealt with are possession offences and three-quarters of those are cannabis possession offences. Now *over half of those cannabis possession offences are cautions.* But it is worth remembering that a caution does bring with it an entry as a criminal record.

It also worth noting that the effect of her report, and of the police 'experiment' in Brixton was to create a form of caution which did not involve a criminal record.

In the same encounter, Dame Ruth compliments the police on being 'very sensible in many ways about their approach to policing the Misuse of Drugs Act. I think without their massive use of discretion, it would have ground to a halt'.

Later still, she says,

At the moment, until our law changes, we have after all for personal use – in theory on the statute book – five years potential imprisonment for a simple possession of cannabis. Now that, I think I am accurate in saying, is more harsh than almost any other country in Europe. *I am not aware that there has ever been a prison sentence of anything approaching that for the simple possession of cannabis. In fact, the average length of a custodial sentence for any possession, including heroin and cocaine, is four months at the moment whereas for heroin and cocaine you could get seven years in theory. So there is a huge gap. One of the good things about the Home Secretary's – as it was stated – possible intention is that it will close the gap between what the law says and what it does* (my italics).[9]

By my calculation her figures mean that even at the end of the last century, roughly 38 per cent of disposals of cannabis cases resulted in nothing more than a caution. Her complaint about this is that it also means a criminal record. She explicitly accepts that people are not going to prison for cannabis possession, and that sentences for the supposedly harder drugs are minimal. She is clearly aware that there is a huge gap between what the law says and what it does, and actually says so. Yet, even while praising the police for their 'discretion', she allows her report to describe this as a 'severe regime'. This simply is not fair dealing, with the public, with politicians or with anyone else.

This truth is even recognised in paragraph 24 of the report itself,

Our recommendation is already accepted, at least tacitly, by the courts. Although the maximum prison sentences for possession under United Kingdom law, from two to seven years, are among the severest in Europe, *they are not, in fact, imposed.* Current sentences

---

[9] BBC News Talking Point Forum, 25 October 2001, <http://news.bbc.co.uk/1/hi/talking_point/forum/1618154.stm>.

for possession are very much shorter at an average of less than 4 months and the evidence suggests that it is unlikely that many of the 4,852 people given custodial sentences for possession offences in 1997 were in prison for the offence of possession alone (my italics).

Interestingly, cannabis possession offences at the time of the report, and after many years of soft policing and soft sentences, stood at 78,000 a year. Since Dame Ruth and Brian Paddick[10] intervened to further weaken the law, these offences have risen to 160,000 a year (2009). Is it possible the two things may be connected?

The extraordinary retreat from punishment is also clearly recorded in the report at paragraph 48. Figures (beginning in the year after Lord Hailsham's 'no prison' speech to magistrates) show that, while in 1974, 3 per cent of all drug offenders (this is not just cannabis, but the 'hard' drugs as well) were cautioned, 12 per cent were immediately imprisoned, 58 per cent were fined, 10 per cent were discharged and 9 per cent received 'community penalties', presumably probation. By 1997, 50 per cent were cautioned, 9 per cent went straight to prison, 22 per cent were fined, and 9 per cent received 'community punishments'. I have left out absolute and conditional discharges and a number of other minor disposals.

The difference is clear. The numbers in 1997 are far higher. In 1974 the total of all drugs offenders was 12,532, in 1997 113,154, more than nine times as many. And the number of cautions had exploded, so that in 1997 almost five times as many people were *cautioned* for drugs offences (56,156) as were *arrested* for drugs offences in 1974 (12,532).

---

[10] pp.196ff.

Runciman and her colleagues are clearly aware of this, and conclude in paragraph 54 that,

> The history of sentencing and penalties associated with drug offences is dominated by two features. First the increasing number of offenders, and second a marked trend over the years towards the use of less formal sanctions and penalties. In particular, the caution is used more, diverting offenders away from the courts.

But this is one of the shortest paragraphs in the whole report, and no conclusions seem to have been drawn from it. Why not? Because these facts run against the whole trend of the document, clearly intended to be a plea for further relaxation. How could this be made, if the report examined these figures properly? How could they fit into their narrative these two facts – that the regime has been growing steadily more liberal, and that during that regime, drugs offences have increased enormously? So it is mentioned enough to satisfy the basic requirements of honesty. But it is not examined.

The report's main recommendations – greater use of cautions, the official end of the use of prison for cannabis possession, the downgrading of cannabis to the lowest possible classification under the 1971 Act, now seem minor and dull. Some supporters of the continuing effort to restrict drug abuse – including this author – were drawn into a futile argument about whether cannabis should be a class 'B' or a class 'C' drug – when the truth is that these gradations have no meaning. Their only real effect is to grant cannabis a special 'soft' status which is dangerously misleading.

But in 2000, the British media were still very much under the illusion that Barbara Wootton *had* been defeated by James Callaghan, and thought these were radical new measures rather than an official confirmation of a quarter of a century of soft justice and soft policing.

The media reaction was remarkable, mainly because several conservative organs were sympathetic. The leak in the *Economist* had of course eased the arrival of the report, since most informed people knew as a result what it would contain and had had time to formulate a view. This author (after 35 years in Fleet Street) believes that there would also have been several private briefings for editors, major commentators and leader-writers, with senior members of the Inquiry made available and perhaps advance copies of the report supplied.

Dame Ruth's greatest and most unexpected success was to secure a far-from-hostile leader in Britain's most socially conservative daily newspaper, the *Daily Mail*. On 29 March 2000, under the headline 'Britain needs a serious debate', the *Mail* said: 'It is clear that the more Government pours money into the battle, the harder police strive and the more rigorously courts enforce the law, the worse the problem becomes'. Noting the rise in drug use since the 1950s, the *Mail* remarked that 'the Police Foundation report calling for a softer line on "recreational" drugs may seem uncomfortably like an admission of defeat. Perhaps that is why the Government dismissed the findings before they were even published'.

The editorial then affirmed that,

> We abhor the taking of drugs. They corrode self-respect, damage minds, harm society and ultimately subvert human dignity. Drugs break up families, destroy lives, perpetuate a despairing underclass and fuel a vast criminal industry, from the street pusher to the gangland trafficker.

But it expressed uncertainty about the role of the police: 'Think how crime figures would fall, if the police didn't have to devote so much time to this problem. This is just one of the compelling reasons for a frank and open public debate on this issue'. Decriminalisation might remove the 'forbidden fruit' attraction, and would undermine the criminal drugs trade.

On the other hand, the *Mail* added,

> Ecstasy kills young people every year and as Leah Betts' mother points out, may cause further tragedies if it is removed from the Class A category. And while some may regard cannabis as no more damaging than alcohol or tobacco, is that really an argument for decriminalisation?

In the article itself, the two sides fight each other to a standstill. But Dame Ruth must have rejoiced at the conclusion:

> Despite this paper's instinctive reservations over a more relaxed approach to softer drugs, we believe that all the arguments on both sides merit hysteria-free and rational examination. The Police Foundation deserves praise for beginning what could and should be a mature and serious national debate.

Calls for 'a debate' on any subject, in the code of modern politics, mean an openness to change. If there were no need to change, there would be nothing to debate. If the *Daily Mail* was open to debate, then the government could feel that an important flank was covered against attack.

The *London Evening Standard*, then a stablemate of the *Daily Mail*, went considerably further. Praising the sagacity, respectability and experience of the Runciman committee, it complained 'It is deplorable ... that the Government should have dismissed the inquiry's findings before they were even published, in a casual statement by a Home Office minister on Sunday'.[11]

---

[11] *Evening Standard*, 28 March 2000.

It said,

> The report argues for a twin-track approach: a tougher line against suppliers, matched by a more discriminating approach to minor users. It makes a clear distinction between 'soft' drugs – cannabis and ecstasy – which do not create dependency, and harder drugs which are unequivocally harmful.

Apart from the arrival of 'Ecstasy' – a drug whose risks seem to me to be quite serious – the policy set out above is exactly the one which Barbara Wootton called for, and which was then enacted and implemented, 30 years before. Amazingly, and quite comically, the 'experts' of the *Standard* are utterly unaware of this as they pronounce their groundbreaking verdict.

Employing the 'what about alcohol and tobacco?' argument which had been in use at least since the long-ago arrest of Donovan, the *Standard* excoriated the Home Office Minister Charles Clarke for not considering

> the obvious comparison with thousands of deaths annually caused by those legal drugs, tobacco and alcohol. Nor does he address the possibility that existing law, by imposing tough penalties for possession of soft and hard drugs alike, encourages young people to regard all illegal substances as interchangeable, and equally valid.

What tough penalties are these? A careful reading of the Runciman report itself[12] would have shown the author that the courts and the police had already gone soft. It appeared that all Runciman wanted to do was formalise and regularise the existing situation.

And then of course there is the declaration that 'The so-called "war against drugs" is being lost'. The evidence given for this is that

---

[12] Especially paragraphs 24 and 25.

drug use in Britain is very high. But what if that is because of the three decades of ever softening enforcement that Dame Ruth had recorded, and proposed to ratify in law?

The greatest joy for the Runciman inquiry must have come from the leading article in the *Daily Telegraph*. The *Telegraph* was no longer the organ of reaction and staidness that most people thought it was. In the Thatcher era, militant economic liberalism and a swaggering foreign policy had supplanted domestic social conservatism, which had all but disappeared from British discourse.

Fleet Street newspapers, including nominally conservative ones, had for some time been recruiting their best writers from the university milieu in which the cause of cannabis was strong and the views of J. S. Mill regarded as unchallengeable. But such changes often go unnoticed by loyal, habitual readers of established newspapers, and the *Telegraph* retained its influence on huge numbers of Conservative politicians and voters. Its verdict was enormously influential.

The paper spoke twice on the subject.[13] First, it said:

> We increasingly incline to the view that the banning of all drugs causes more harm than good. People like substances that alter their mood, and only strict puritans believe that they should never use any of them. A cup of coffee, a glass of wine or beer, even the odd cigarette are among the legitimate pleasures of life. The reason that they do not do much harm is that they have been socialised – they are surrounded by customs and manners and jokes and friendship and all the things which make life tolerable. Alcohol and tobacco remain lethal, and alcohol, unlike tobacco, has the power to destroy the character of the person who uses it:

---

[13] *Daily Telegraph*, 30 March 2000.

it does so for tens of thousands of people in this country every year.

Drugs, the *Telegraph* went on, are – despite all their dangers – not 'fundamentally different' from alcohol and tobacco. 'Given that we live in an age in which the drugs of the world have found their way to our shores, surely the truly conservative answer to the problem is to find ways of acclimatising drugs to bourgeois society rather than yelling vainly into the wind'.

A few days later it had another go,[14] declaring that the Home Secretary Jack Straw had 'misjudged the public's mood on whether there should be a debate on the legalisation of cannabis'. Straw had made it known that he would ignore most of the Runciman committee's proposals; a 'poorly judged' response, according to the *Telegraph*:

> It is clear that the report asked sufficiently important questions to warrant a public debate and not a knee-jerk dismissal from the Government. The surge in drug-related crimes, the fact that cannabis has now crossed the generation gap, and the evidence of its use as a valuable palliative in terminal illness, all make a debate necessary.

Once again, the apparently neutral call for 'a debate' is code for changes to the existing law and practice – and in a liberal direction. The unthinking acceptance of the belief that crime is caused by harsh law enforcement rather than the opposite, and the swallowing of the dubious case for 'medical marijuana', show the mind of the writer. Once again, the newspaper does not appear to have noticed the report's own admission that the softening sought by Dame Ruth had already been in progress for 30 years.

---

[14] *Daily Telegraph*, 3 April 2000.

With equal grandeur, and competing for the crown of Sir Simon Jenkins, the *Financial Times*'s Martin Wolf told his audience of bankers and businessmen to get down with the kids[15] – not that London's cocaine-snorting business classes were by then any sort of conservative stronghold.

Seizing the wrong end of the stick in firm hands, Mr Wolf thundered:

> Last week, a beacon of sanity was shone on British policy towards illicit drugs. The source was a committee established by the Police Foundation, under the chairmanship of Lady Runciman. Its recommendations are as moderate as its membership is respectable.

Had he actually studied them with any care? Apparently not. He of course quoted the words 'As the report notes, the UK "has a more severe regime of control over possession offences than most of the other European countries which we have studied"'.

He noted the numbers of arrests:

> 1997, 86,034 people were dealt with for offences involving cannabis, a rise of 114 per cent since 1990. There were also more than 1 million 'stop and searches' in England and Wales in 1993–97, resulting in 134,500 arrests, again mostly for cannabis.

But he seems not have noticed how these cases ended and what penalties, if any, followed. Had he done so, his argument would have lost most of its force. There is also the old Donovan and Gipsy Dave argument about how much more dangerous alcohol is, an argument so trivial, mistaken and dense that a first-year undergraduate could see through it – if he wanted to see through it. Yet this is one of the grandest writers in one of the grandest newspapers in the land.

---

[15] *Financial Times*, 3 April 2000.

One rather less grand commentator, Toby Young, actually said something a good deal more candid. Condemning the Police Foundation's recommended softening of the law, Mr Young confessed to being a past cannabis smoker, and dismissed the almost universally accepted argument that marijuana is less dangerous than the bogeyman drugs, heroin and cocaine:[16]

> To distinguish between these drugs according to the different amounts of harm they cause, as the Foundation sought to do, is completely spurious since cannabis, in its own way, is every bit as harmful as cocaine and heroin. To paraphrase Allen Ginsberg, I've seen the best minds of my generation destroyed by marijuana.

He continued:

> No sensible person could seriously believe that cocaine is more dangerous than cannabis. As someone who's taken both in copious quantities, let me assure Runciman that the opposite is the case. Dope blighted my adolescence, transforming me from a bright, energetic teenager into a moronic, lethargic waster. For five years the only things I read were Fabulous Furry Freak Brothers comics and Zen and the Art of Motorcycle Maintenance. Cocaine has done nothing more damaging than burn a hole in my wallet.

Next, Young ridiculed the 'medical benefits' of marijuana:

> At one time or other, morphine, laudanum, cocaine, nicotine, alcohol and LSD have all been touted as medicine. A few years ago, a *New Republic* journalist who attended the opening of a 'medical marijuana' clinic in San Francisco discovered that the conditions for which California doctors can now legitimately

---

[16] *Observer*, 2 April 2000.

prescribe cannabis include Aids, cancer, epilepsy, sciatica, 'eye problems', insomnia, anxiety, depression, 'stress management', headaches, impotence, 'writer's cramp' and 'recovering lost memories'.

As a reformed dope fiend, I must confess to being a member of that tiny minority for whom marijuana use was not medical. Insomnia, anxiety, depression, stress, headaches? It certainly gave me all of those. As for recovering lost memories ... sorry, what was that again?

This article stands out as one of the most enjoyably sensible written on the subject – though it is important to add that Mr Young was lucky not to end up, as did Henry Cockburn[17] in the locked ward of a mental hospital, a fate which was almost certainly brought about by heavy adolescent use of supposedly 'safe', 'soft' cannabis. And it is only fair to add that Mr Young ended by calling for the decriminalisation of almost anything, in an argument that may or may not have been Swiftian:

So let's not pretend dope is any less harmful than Class As ... Provided they're taken in moderation, cocaine and heroin are no more dangerous than cannabis and E. The Police Foundation should recommend the decriminalisation of all four.[18]

What, then, did Runciman suggest? There were 81 recommendations in all, but the chief ones were the scrapping of powers to arrest and imprison cannabis users and the introduction of ticket-style fixed penalties for soft drug offences. One member of

---

[17] p.19.
[18] In case Mr Young was not being satirical, I would agree that they are all equally dangerous in their own separate ways, though the cannabis risk, an unpredictable threat to mental health, is perhaps the most terrifying of these hazards. But I would add that in that case they should all be equally, strictly illegal.

the panel, Denis O'Connor, objected to the other major suggestion, the placing of cannabis in class 'C'. He plainly saw that this was politically difficult, though it would in fact be implemented by the New Labour government not long afterwards. The committee also urged that the bulk of the state's drugs budget should no longer go on enforcing the law, but mainly on the education and treatment of drug users.

In a large sop to the pro-drug lobby, they urged that alcohol should be a class 'A' drug and tobacco a class 'C' drug, plainly propagandist recommendations with no practical application, which might have been designed to blur the distinction between legal drugs and illegal ones.

As usual in documents urging easier treatment for drug users, the 'wicked' dealers, the use of whose wicked product is either not a crime, or is a matter for active sympathy, there were recommendations for harsher sentences for cannabis supply – up from five years in prison to seven. This illogical, indeed contradictory view mirrors very closely the similar provisions in the 1971 Act. Runciman also sympathised with the campaign for 'medical' cannabis, urging that its 'medicinal' use should be legal.

This was a significant advance on the Wootton Report, and one that would grow in importance over years to come. The claim that cannabis has valuable medical properties had not been a major part of the legalisation campaign at the time of the Wootton Report, but had since become one. Runciman's report concluded absurdly (given the grave lack of objective knowledge on the subject, then or since) that cannabis itself was relatively harmless. She also wanted an end to prosecutions of owners of premises where it was smoked. But, as those who wish to weaken the drug laws to the point of inanity always do, the document covered itself by declaring 'There is no question of our recommending legalisation of any of these drugs'.

This statement is of course technically completely accurate. The proposed changes remained cunningly within Britain's Treaty obligations. But it gave a wholly misleading impression of the changes which would – with some speed – result from its implementation. If something is not, in practice illegal, then how is that different from it being legal?

20

Legislation on the beat – Brian Paddick

Conservative middle-class people often say that the laws against cannabis threaten to 'criminalise' young people. The logic of this claim is idiotic. Nobody is forced to take or buy cannabis. It is known to be against the law. If someone buys it or uses it, he criminalises himself. But such advocates cannot quite bring themselves to attack the law, so they pretend that the law is attacking them. They are generally respectable professional types, and are usually afraid on behalf of their own children, who have been brought up – by culturally radical parents who have themselves used cannabis – to believe that the drug is perfectly safe and respectable. They do not want their sons' and daughters' happy and ambitious lives and careers to be thwarted or disrupted by a criminal conviction. But they do not see why they should stop smoking cannabis. What they actually mean is that they do not accept this law.

But their concern is greatly overdone. The chances of any respectable young person being prosecuted for cannabis possession are very small. But that is only the half of it.

Late in 2010 I had a broadcast clash with Professor David Nutt, the expert in Neuropsychopharmacology.[1] He has been for some years a prominent campaigner for weakening Britain's drug laws and was for some time a principal government adviser on the law and member of the Advisory Council on the Misuse of Drugs, the permanent body which keeps the 1971 law under constant (and constantly liberal) review.

He asserted, in support of a claim that the existing law was harming young people, that '160,000 people were given criminal sanctions for possessing cannabis'.

I replied confidently that if so most of them were not actually punished. I was sure this was the case. But when I researched his claim I found that I was even more right than I had thought. In 2009[2] 162, 610 cannabis cases were handled by police in England and Wales. Of these, 19,137 cases were dealt with through police 'cautions', which expire after three months and need not normally be declared to employers – a way of dealing with cannabis which dates back to 1991. 11,492 resulted in Penalty Notices for Disorder, an on-the-spot rebuke which generally results in no punishment of any kind, which are recorded indefinitely. A mere 22,478 cases actually ended in court and many of them did so because they were only one of several charges against the defendant. The outcome of several thousand more arrests was simply not recorded and cannot be traced, an extraordinary fact in a modern, computerised country.

But the most significant and interesting figure was that 86,953 were dealt with by a procedure known as a 'cannabis warning'. This is a curious anomaly. Though it is recommended as the preferred response by ACPO, it has no legal status.

It is not recorded centrally. A person could receive such a warning

---

[1] p.140.
[2] The latest year for which I have been able to obtain these very hard-to-find figures.

in several different jurisdictions, without the information being shared. It does not create a criminal record. No Act of Parliament mentions it. How did this highly significant legal change come about? I asked several government departments and the ACPO. They were unable to give me a clear answer.

After some study of the archives, it became clear that an extraordinary thing had happened. The police themselves had taken to making the law, instead of just enforcing it.

In earlier chapters I recorded how the 1971 Misuse of Drugs Act was – uniquely in English law – a sort of work in progress, moving inch by inch towards almost total decriminalisation of cannabis in a process that has already lasted more than 40 years. It had begun by taking the decisive step of separating cannabis from other drugs, and distinguishing between possession and trafficking. But this was only the beginning.

Somewhere in the heart of government, whichever party was in power, the supporters of liberalisation continued to work for their end. The existence of an 'Advisory' council or committee on the 'Misuse of Drugs' kept the subject under constant review. The review was a ratchet, operating in one direction only. This was the 'further research' called for by the original Wootton Report. When a social and moral conservative, Dr Hans-Christian Raabe, was for once appointed to the Committee in 2011, he was swiftly removed on wholly irrelevant grounds (namely, shaky accusations that he held unacceptable views on homosexuality).

The continued weakening of the law followed this course: In 1973, magistrates were told that – though the Act still formally allowed it – nobody should be sent to prison for mere cannabis possession.[3] Meanwhile, egged on by the various officially sponsored Advisory

---

[3] p.141.

Councils and Committees which keep this law under constant review, the maximum penalties for possession were whittled down to such an extent that by 1994, a senior police officer could openly state that cannabis possession was now decriminalised,[4] and tell the Home Secretary that it would be foolish to revert to higher penalties. The Home Secretary did not do so. On the contrary, the process of diluting the law continued to its present state.

The police, as also discussed above, had become strong advocates of weakening the law on drugs. Enforcing it was a complicated and time-consuming nuisance with few rewards for them. It made them unpopular and it also led to them being accused of racial prejudice in some urban zones where the cannabis trade was dominated by ethnic minorities. This, though nobody mentioned it, was a direct result of the neutering of the penalties for possession, and the law's absurd view that possession was somehow less of an offence than trafficking. If police arrests and prosecutions had resulted in severe penalties, then their actions would have a deterrent effect. But arrests and prosecutions which end with feeble penalties undermine the law.

In 2001, an enterprising and original senior policeman, presumably with the covert support of his superiors, decided to stretch the law still further. His name is Brian Paddick. I know Mr Paddick, who is now a Liberal Democrat politician, and believe that he is a serious person who was acting with honesty and integrity for what he believed to be a good end. I happen to disagree strongly with him. But what follows is not a criticism of Mr Paddick, who was doing what he thought right with energy, diligence and competence, in the belief that his superiors – at the very least – wished him well. It is a criticism of the way drugs law is made in this country.

And how is it made? It is made by the police taking the law into

---

[4] p.159.

their own hands instead of enforcing it without fear or favour, and by a carefully briefed media campaign.

On 27 March 2001, the London *Evening Standard* reported under the headline 'New Soft Line on Cannabis' that London police were launching a 'radical new initiative' whereby

> Rather than arresting people found with small amounts of cannabis, police would simply issue a warning and confiscate the drugs ... Senior officers in Brixton – the capital's premier illegal drugs market – are planning the move in an effort to free their resources to fight harder drugs such as crack cocaine. Lambeth officers deny the policy would turn Brixton into a new Amsterdam. They believe the strategy would curb drugs sales by giving officers more time on the streets to pursue dealers and customers.

Brian Paddick, the new Commander in charge of Lambeth policing, was quoted as saying:

> We are seriously considering using this formal warning process to deal with cannabis possession ... This new move will not turn Brixton into a mini-Amsterdam. In Amsterdam the police don't take small amounts of cannabis off you. Here, we will.

Paddick added that the confiscations would disrupt the criminal market.

He ended by comparing cannabis possession to illegal parking, or perhaps shoplifting, offences regarded in modern Britain as so trivial they barely warrant the attention of the criminal law:

> Brixton is known as a place to come and buy drugs. But if we move to this policy of formal warnings, the message will be that you may be able to come and buy – but you might not be able to leave with your purchases. It might put them off coming here to buy in the first place.

Police (the *Standard* continued),

> regularly give members of the public similar warnings for minor offences which can be recorded in a book. The practice is often used for shoplifting, for example. Similarly, drivers can get a warning for illegal parking, or people can be moved on for being drunk in the street.

This newspaper story is in effect the opening speech in a debate (though there will be hardly any opposing speeches). But the debate took place in the media, and among the police, not in Parliament.

The following day the *Daily Mail* (one of very few newspapers not by then in favour of decriminalising cannabis, though it had shown some sympathy to the Runciman report) recorded some objections. One came from Mrs Janet Betts whose teenage daughter Leah had died horribly after taking Ecstasy. Such victims of the drug culture are allowed by the media to speak passionately against it, as their suffering makes it hard for them to be dismissed or mocked as other anti-drug campaigners are. But while they are treated with personal respect because of their bereavement, there is also a tendency to discount what they say as no more than understandable emotion.

She accurately observed, 'It's one more step along the road to legalisation'. And she added 'I've had Tony Blair and drugs czar Keith Hellawell tell me it's not their policy to legalise anything ever, but I think it's coming'.

She added perceptively 'It's easier than prosecuting and the crime rate would drop like a stone'.

A Tory MP Gerald Howarth, a member of the Commons Home Affairs Committee, said:

> It all seems to suggest that the police are being overwhelmed by

the problem of drugs and are having to choose between the lesser of two evils.

But the result will be that people in possession of dangerous drugs are effectively going to be allowed to carry on their way with only a mild rap on the knuckles.

That is the wrong signal to send out. In the absence of the legalisation of cannabis – which I would wholly oppose – it must be cracked down on.

As the story of Ann Widdecombe[5] makes plain, calls for 'crackdowns' on drugs were, by then, no longer likely to get much of a hearing in high-level British politics. The real influence was elsewhere. However loudly politicians shouted (as they had since the days of James Callaghan) that they were 'tough' on drugs, they were in fact secretly willing to let the laws shrivel away. The real influence lay not with the noisy figure of Miss Widdecombe, but with the steely pro-decriminalisation lobbyist Dame Ruth.[6]

The flow of opinion was by then all going the other way. Paul Barker wrote approvingly in the *Evening Standard* of 29 March 2001:

> The Metropolitan Police is being more responsive to public opinion, in one terrain at least, than this obsessively poll-reading Government. It's an inversion of the usual pattern: an encouraging version of the 'Man bites dog' story. Commander Brian Paddick, who has recently taken charge of policing Lambeth, has said that, from now on, his officers won't automatically arrest someone found in possession of small amounts of cannabis.

As Mr Barker realised, the proposals were an application of what the

---

[5] Dealt with on pp.163–9.
[6] pp.171–92.

Runciman report had concluded. The report, Barker reminded the reader,

> was rubbished by ministers at the time. To this day, at the Home Office, Charles Clarke, the minister in charge of drugs policy, rejects the slightest whiff of reform. Last month the Government's 10-year plan for improving the criminal justice system ignored the Runciman recommendations totally ... It was head-in-sand time.

After making the usual obligatory claim that this retreat would enable police to concentrate on really harmful offences, Barker suggested that Commander Paddick was not acting on his own. He explained,

> The Home Office regularly speaks of Sir John Stevens, Sir Paul Condon's lower-profile successor as Metropolitan Police Commissioner, as a 'white knight'. He is seen as leading the battle against crime, racism and heaven knows what else. But the white knight is galloping away from the party line. Sir John himself has said that cannabis possession isn't a priority crime for the Met.
>
> Contrary to its critics' allegation, the Runciman report didn't recommend legalisation. But it did recommend a scaling-down of some unreasonably fierce penalties, most notably for having small amounts of cannabis. It said this should no longer be an arrestable offence.

Observantly, Mr Barker contrasts the stance of elected politicians with that of the actual machinery of government.

At the time,[7] it looked as though the Government might just be

---

[7] Of the Runciman report.

batting the report into the long grass until it had got an election out of the way, when common sense might again prevail. But, no. In Millbank's massive election guide to how Labour candidates should answer any awkward questions, they've just been told to say No to any prospect of change. Enter common sense, stage right, from an unexpected quarter. The Met is disentangling one of the many criminal justice knots the Government has got itself into.

In any case, the new policy went ahead at the end of June 2001, a six-month 'pilot scheme' described in an *Evening Standard* report on 18 June as 'a desperate effort to free officers' time to deal with more serious crime'. It is astonishing how often this spin is placed on this policy. But such repetition is effective. I have heard the same explanation on the lips of 70-year-old members of the ultra-Conservative Monday Club, all of whom thought it was their own idea. The same report explained that the police reasoning had taken on a liberal, amoral tone: 'In an internal police report Mr Paddick, 42, outlined how the arrest and "criminalisation" of people for possession of the drug was raising concern in the local community – it was often the spark to light possible racial conflicts'.

And it described how the police had simply decided to follow a course which – if anyone else had done it – they would have described as 'taking the law into their own hands'.

Mr Paddick said: 'Based on what the courts are saying on the seriousness of possession of cannabis I decided that one of the things that we should do was to stop arresting people for cannabis. It is an extremely bureaucratic and therefore expensive process to get a conviction. As these figures show, having gone through all that bureaucracy people are being fined between £20 and £50 or being conditionally discharged'.

The demand for change was also coming from police officers

on patrol in Lambeth who were routinely coming across cannabis. On their own initiative they had already adopted an informal policy of warning people and getting them to put the drugs 'down the drain'.

While they were doing this, in line with many other boroughs, the Met was also developing one of the strictest anticorruption disciplines of any force and undercover officers were routinely mounting integrity tests against colleagues suspected of corruption.

In Brixton the officers on the ground were increasingly concerned that they could fall victim to an integrity test if they informally confiscated drugs without going through the correct procedure of arrest and charge. So, they approached Mr Paddick with a request for a formal policy which would allow them to continue to deal with cannabis in a more relaxed way.

But there were some interesting signs of nervousness. Perhaps alarmed by Mr Barker's earlier suggestions that the policy had high-level backing, an unnamed source had briefed the reporters that the opposite was true: 'The commander[8] decided to take a leaf out of the political spin doctors' book and float the policy first in the Evening Standard to test reaction to the on-the-spot warning scheme'. He had not consulted his immediate superiors, or even Commissioner Sir John Stevens. As the *Standard* piece remarked, this was quite a gamble, but Scotland Yard had now conducted a review and approved of the scheme:

> Mr Paddick refuses to discuss the details of how the policy won over his superiors at Scotland Yard ... All Mr Paddick will say is the policy has the backing of the Commissioner and has won overwhelming support from the community and most politicians.

---

[8] Brian Paddick.

This is a very curious account. Did an Area Commander (a position less exalted than it sounds) really have the power to embark on an experiment of this kind without support from the highest level? Was Britain's largest and most political police force so decentralised? Or were senior officials simply leaving themselves an escape route in case the experiment went badly wrong? It is curious that no identifiable individual is directly quoted in support of the claim that Commander Paddick was acting on his own. This usually means that a briefing has been given at high level, by someone seeking to influence the coverage of a politically important event. But if it were true, why would nobody go on the record to say so?

The answer is given in what follows in the same article:

> Since the initiative was launched, the Home Office issued a statement saying its policy was always to allow police officers discretion to caution people for possession of small amounts of cannabis. However, it said that the Home Office wished to see a uniform approach to cannabis across the country. The Association of Chief Police Officers has been equally cautious, saying simply that it would wait and see the results of the pilot scheme.

So the Home Office[9] saw the project as an opportunity to get a 'uniform approach' across the country – but one that would be *de facto* and did not involve any actual legislation. Mr Paddick would be praised and promoted if all went without a scandal, and dumped if it went wrong.

A few weeks later, Britain's single most influential lobbyist for drug decriminalisation threw himself into the hurly burly. Sir Simon

---

[9] In those days not yet split into two departments, one for policing and another in charge of the justice system.

Jenkins, who combines a sober and conservative manner, style and appearance with way-out 1960s ideas, told *Evening Standard* readers on 5 July:

> The 1971 Misuse of Drugs Act, unreformed by Michael Howard and Jack Straw when Home Secretaries, has made London the most lucrative and drug-ridden city in Europe. Statistics may be unreliable, but the recent National Criminal Intelligence Survey reports that cannabis, cocaine and heroin are now more plentiful and cheaper in London than ever, and than anywhere.

This is a little disingenuous. The Act might have been unreformed by those two Ministers, but Sir Simon must have known how much it had been diluted since 1971.

He continues with an extraordinary, utterly contradictory statement, which beautifully sums up the thought-free, fact-denying absurdity of his position – which is the position of all those who burble that 'the War on Drugs has failed'.

He first says that 'No product in the world is more intensively and successfully marketed door-to-door than illegal drugs in Britain'.[10]

He then goes on to pronounce without qualification that 'The Misuse of Drugs Act has failed completely'. This is a very interesting statement. What does he mean by it? If the veteran pro-decriminalisation campaigner Mr Stephen Abrams (cited many times above) is correct, the purpose of the Misuse of Drugs Act was to move in the direction of decriminalising cannabis possession. Yet this was done behind a screen of militant anti-drug rhetoric, which successfully

---

[10] Though is hard to establish whether these drugs really outperform milk, say, or pizza, in this area.

fooled such acute commentators as Ronald Butt. Has it also fooled Sir Simon?

It seems so. He appears actually to believe that the 1971 Act was a measure of stern prohibition. For he says 'Introduced by Sir Edward Heath, it will rank with American Prohibition as an all-time classic of counterproductive legislation'.

Appearing to misunderstand completely the actual operation of the law, Sir Simon concludes that a) the 1971 Act involved harsh prohibition, b) it has failed, and so c) it is absurd to carry on criminalising supply if criminalising demand has not worked.

He argues:

The police are told to concentrate on suppressing the supply of drugs whose consumption is accepted as ubiquitous. This is merely to move from one nonsense to another. While some users undoubtedly commit crimes to maintain their 'habit', most pay for drugs from normal income. The social menace lies in the criminalisation of supply. As long as there is demand, and demand is massive and endemic, there will be supply. The question is simple.

And so he proposes the following hippy dream:

London must get used to legal conduits for the drugs trade through bars, shops and pharmacies. It must join much of the rest of Europe in re-establishing the pre-1971 controlled prescription of heroin, with free needle exchange and treatment. It must accept that cocaine is the drug of choice for hundreds of thousands of otherwise law-abiding young people, but it must be taxed, made more costly and quality controlled.

In short, the government must itself become part of the trade in narcotics, and the British exchequer be corrupted with taxes on narcotics. The United Kingdom must become a Narco-State.

This inverted pyramid of wild libertarian radicalism (so unhinged that even New Labour and David Cameron have not –yet – enacted or supported it) is balanced upon one wholly false premise – the ignorant belief that the 1971 Act entails harsh prohibition and enforcement. If this is not so, and it is not, then everything else that Sir Simon says is based on a profound misunderstanding. It is precisely because of this repeated error, made again and again by people who – like Sir Simon Jenkins – really ought to know better, that I have written this book.

For, while no present politician could enact Sir Simon's plan, his incessant pro-legalisation articles provide cover for what amounts to the same thing, a law against drugs so feebly enforced that it might as well not exist. As long as loud and influential voices are constantly raised against alleged 'prohibition' and the fantasy is maintained that there is a 'war against drugs', three things will continue happening. Politicians will continue to seek to appear 'tough' by rejecting any clear and open legislation to decriminalise drugs. The police and the criminal justice system will continue to dilute the 1971 Act so that ever-increasing amounts of ever more highly classified drugs will not attract the attention of the law; and those who seek to correct the real mistake in national policy will be excluded from the debate.

Meanwhile, those who make these shrill and ill-informed calls will be widely praised for their supposed courage and forward thinking.

The continuing story of the Brixton experiment shows this process in operation.

By October of 2001, the Paddick project was already being described as a success. And the then Home Secretary, David Blunkett, was providing cover for a national extension of the 'Cannabis Warning', by regrading cannabis as a Class 'C' drug. These classifications, as discussed elsewhere, are scientifically meaningless and have no real objective foundation. They appear to have been invented in

1971, purely so as to distinguish cannabis from heroin and LSD. Now they were being used to justify a sort of policing Dunkirk – a mass withdrawal by defeated officers of the law from any further effort to enforce the law against cannabis, its true nature masked as a triumph by clever propaganda.

The fact was that the source and origin of their defeat was the allegedly draconian 1971 Act and its Home Office guardians, aided by various other easily led public figures from Dame Ruth's 'Police Foundation' to the House of Commons Home Affairs Committee, not to mention the various incarnations of the Advisory Council on the Misuse of Drugs, originally an 'Advisory Committee'.

The *Evening Standard* reported confidently on 24 October 2001, in terms which must have delighted all drug liberalisers:

> When David Blunkett's move to relax the law on cannabis comes into force next year, Scotland Yard officers will claw back more than 74,000 hours a year currently spent dealing with arrests for trivial amounts of soft drugs. And while London will benefit from the equivalent of an extra 26 officers on duty to fight crime every day, courts in the capital will also stand to gain savings running into tens of millions of pounds a year.

Note the use of such words as 'trivial' amounts and 'soft' drugs, both judgements open to debate. Note also the manipulative portrayal of a retreat from law-enforcement as a move to liberate police to concentrate on other unspecified crime. Who is to say how the time will be used? Will anyone ever check?

The newspaper added,

> But while the Home Secretary will be credited as the politician who had the courage to recognise that the cannabis laws needed reform, the change is a personal triumph for Lambeth borough

police chief Commander Brian Paddick, who took it upon himself to put common sense before a law which was failing his community.

Mr Paddick was getting his reward – which would eventually lead to his appointment as Deputy Assistant Commissioner.

So was Ruth Runciman. The article went on to report that the government would probably be able to change the law by spring:

> Yesterday's unheralded announcement – welcomed by police leaders, drugs charities, and Opposition MPs – marks a startling shift in government thinking. In March last year, Dame Ruth Runciman's thoughtful Police Foundation report on drugs and the law – a two-year study involving academics, police officers and health experts – called for cannabis to be downgraded.

What was the 'startling shift' in government thinking mentioned here? It is not explained. That is because it did not exist. The Brixton policy was a direct continuation of 30 years of discreet salami-slicing, by which cannabis was gradually decriminalised.

Another indication of the true state of affairs came in November 2001 when several senior police officers gave evidence to MPs on their attitude to drugs. The *Daily Mail* reported:

> Police chiefs were accused of abandoning the war on drugs last night after demanding an astonishing softening of the law. One senior officer called for Ecstasy to be reclassified as a 'soft drug'. He also supported the idea of Government backed 'shooting galleries' where heroin addicts could inject themselves without fear of arrest. Another top policeman said he had no interest in arresting weekend users of Ecstasy and cocaine and that cannabis should be completely legalised.

The *Mail* actually described the Association of Chief Police Officers as 'the national policymaking body', an accurate assessment but not a fact generally acknowledged.

It recounted how,

> in a written statement, ACPO admitted that the Government's strategy had failed to turn the tide of rising drug use, deaths and drug-related violent crime. Then two senior Scotland Yard officers spelt out to the Commons Home Affairs Select Committee how far the police leadership is now prepared to go towards legalising drugs.

The word 'admitted' is important here. Like the imprisonment of criminals, the laws against drugs are a policy the governing elite loathe and despise, but feel they are forced to follow by public opinion. Because of this strange anomaly, officials in charge of both of these policies are allowed, if not encouraged, to be fiercely publicly critical of their outcomes.

By January 2002 the *Evening Standard* was reporting that Mr Paddick's experiment was a success, and was being extended. It reported that, after six months of the Brixton pilot scheme, 'more than 400 drug users have escaped prosecution for possessing cannabis'. Moreover, the initiative 'is estimated to have saved 2,000 hours of police time freeing officers to concentrate on arrests for crack and heroin supply. It has also saved potential court costs of £4 million'.

The following figures were given: 'From July to November 2000, 278 people were arrested for possession in Lambeth. In the same period last year, 381 were cautioned for possessing the drug, rising to an expected 400 by the end of December'.

Other police forces, the *Standard* added, had warned that 'cautions may allow dealers off the hook because searches of home addresses, where more evidence of abuse may be found, are not carried out'.

Paddick said the scheme was going well, but a few weeks later came the first serious sign of opposition. Interestingly, it came not from among senior police officers but from a leader of ordinary constables, far less penetrated by liberal philosophies than the senior ranks of the force. This was Fred Broughton, chairman of the Police Federation, who raised serious objections to the scheme in his evidence to the Home Affairs Select Committee. As the *Standard* reported, Mr Broughton's argued that the Lambeth project 'had led to a surge in the number of users and a growth in hard drugs' and gave children the impression cannabis use had been condoned by the authorities'.

He told the Select Committee:

> There's anecdotal evidence in south London that more people are involving themselves in cannabis. There's also anecdotal evidence that more serious matters – crack abusers and crack dealers – are becoming more visible and active.

But not long afterwards the other side produced their rebuttal. I have recorded these accounts in some detail as they are the closest we have to a Parliamentary debate of one of the biggest policy changes made on drugs in modern British history. Parliament and the voters, as is so often with social policy, had no role in the change. It was never in any Party manifesto nor submitted to any sort of electoral test, like the major social reforms of the 1960s with which it is linked.

On 20 March the *Standard* said,

> The 'softly softly' drugs policies of Brian Paddick … have resulted in more arrests for hard drugs and a fall in street crime.
>
> New figures which appear to vindicate the Brixton drugs experiment also show that burglary is down.

Drug arrests in Lambeth borough, which includes Brixton, rose 65 per cent in a year after Commander Paddick decided not to arrest cannabis users, saying the tactic would allow officers more time to pursue dealers in heroin and crack cocaine.

The report was accompanied with some perfectly amazing statistics, which seemed to show that the policy was not simply successful but actually flawless:

There were 159 class A drug arrests in Lambeth last month compared with 96 for both cannabis and class A drugs in the similar period last year.

Street crime has been cut by 35 per cent and burglaries by eight per cent.

Crucially, the findings refute critics' claims that the new policy has attracted even more drug dealing and use in the borough. Arrests for class A drugs rose from 90 last December to 107 in January and 159 last month. Street robberies, which were running at more than 30 a day in Lambeth in the aftermath of the 11 September bombings, when many officers were redeployed to central London, have been cut to 17 a day.

The corresponding figure for last year is 23 a day.

Burglaries, many of which are drug-related, have been cut to 363 last month from 397 in February last year.

Could there be any better news? There could:

Since the introduction of the no-arrest cannabis policy last summer, burglaries have dropped by 26 per cent and street crime – a major problem in Lambeth – has fallen six per cent.

Sources say up to 2,500 police man-hours have been saved by removing the bureaucratic requirements on officers making arrests for cannabis.

Such figures, like all politically important statistics, are of course open to question. Arrests themselves are not a sign of success. If you stop arresting people for a crime, there will axiomatically be fewer arrests, but this does not show that crime has diminished. Many crimes, street robberies and burglaries included, are not always reported in areas where they are common and people are not insured. So they exist outside official statistics, and neither police nor government are especially anxious to seek the information out by other means. A variation in burglaries, between 397 and 363 a month, does not demonstrate a long-term trend. And who could have blamed the Metropolitan Police if they had not made a special effort to ensure that the cannabis experiment was a 'success' in terms of statistics?

I pointed out earlier that all crimes are, in a way, caused by laws, and if you have fewer laws, or do not enforce them, you will have less crime. But you will not necessarily have less trouble, less human wickedness or less grief.

Then, in early April, came a statistical counterblast, again reported in the *Evening Standard*:

> The controversial Lambeth cannabis experiment has suffered a setback, with new figures showing the scheme has led to a flood of people into the area to deal in drugs.
>
> Official statistics released by Scotland Yard show a 13 per cent rise in the number of dealers and drug users moving into the borough during the first six months of the pilot last year.
>
> Scotland Yard said the results showed there was a 'downside' to the project that allows people caught in possession of cannabis merely to be cautioned and have their drugs confiscated rather than be prosecuted.
>
> Deputy Assistant Commissioner Mike Fuller, the new head

of Scotland Yard's Drugs Directorate, said *there was no question the scheme would be abandoned* but a number of issues needed to be resolved before it was expanded across London (my italics).

Perhaps the most striking part of the story was that Mr Fuller said that there was 'no question' of abandoning the scheme. If that was so – and I think it was – then how genuine a trial was it? Or was its result fixed in advance?

The details that followed were not encouraging. From 1 July to 31 December 2000, the police investigated 118 allegations of drug supply in Lambeth, 45 per cent involving people from the borough and 55 involving visitors. During the previous year's pilot scheme, on the other hand, there were 143 allegations of drug supply. The figure for visitors to Lambeth increased to 62 per cent. The *Standard* commented:

> Until now, the pilot scheme has been considered a success in saving police time. A study showed the policy saved 1,350 hours of officer time – the equivalent of nearly two extra officers – and a further 1,150 hours of civil staff time in preparing cases. Police in Lambeth also recorded 35 per cent more cannabis possession offences and 11 per cent more trafficking-offences in the six months of the scheme compared to the same period the previous year. In adjoining boroughs, possession offences fell by 4 per cent and trafficking by 34 per cent.
>
> Critics of the scheme argue this also shows more people were visiting Lambeth to take and deal in drugs.
>
> Mr Fuller said: 'The new work has borne out the anecdotal evidence that there were more dealers and other drug users coming into the area as a result of the pilot.
>
> 'We know that some of that was out of ignorance about the

policy, with people mistakenly believing that drugs had been legalised in Lambeth'.

Were they in fact mistaken? The difference between the policy and legalisation is purely technical. The effect is the same.

He insisted (once again showing that this was an experiment intended to succeed):

> This shows there are downsides to the scheme but *it does not put the scheme in doubt*. It has saved time and it has freed up officers to carry out other work. What is hard to show is if that extra time has been spent on tackling class 'A' drugs, which is the aim of the pilot (my italics).

Mr Fuller added: 'our main concern is about sending out mixed messages to young people about drugs. Even if cannabis is reclassified it will remain a criminal offence'.

It is easy to see why he was concerned about this. Young people can see the practical operation of such a policy quite clearly, and can swiftly conclude that cannabis possession does not really remain a criminal offence. This is obvious. *But it cannot ever be openly avowed by any senior official person.*

In May, there was another hiccup. The *Mail on Sunday* reported:

> One of Scotland Yard's most senior officers has admitted there are 'significant flaws' in the softly, softly approach to cannabis pioneered by Commander Brian Paddick.
>
> Deputy Assistant Commissioner Michael Fuller said the scheme, which sees police no longer prosecuting for cannabis possession, had attracted more drug dealers to the trial area, Lambeth in South London.
>
> It had also resulted in children arriving for school 'stoned'. It is

the first time an officer of such high rank has publicly expressed doubts about the scheme.

Writing in the magazine *Police Review*, DAC Fuller says: 'Our school officers report that children feel that the police are sending mixed messages to young people, by on the one hand trying to deter them from abusing and experimenting with drugs and yet appearing hypocritical by not strictly enforcing the drug laws.

One vicar in Brixton reported children arriving at school in the mornings stoned through smoking cannabis.

Many parents of teenagers are raising concerns with me that the current perception of liberalisation and relaxation of the drug laws created by the scheme will inevitably result in more young people (and adults) experimenting in using cannabis and possibly harder drugs'.

Mr Fuller also admitted that there was still plenty of paperwork under the new scheme.

Unfortunately for the advocates of the soft-on-cannabis scheme, the area involved was (and still is) represented in Parliament by an alert, independent-minded and socially conservative Labour MP, Kate Hoey. Ms Hoey was not convinced, and was prepared to protest.

She said, in an article for the *Mail on Sunday*,

> Brian Paddick no doubt had the best of intentions when he introduced the experiment. But, in my view, it has seriously undermined law and order, reduced police morale and crucially led to an increased use of drugs by young people.

She quoted a volunteer who described the situation thus: 'The dealers have got rid of the police here, now they want rid of those of us who are prepared to speak out', and pointed out,

> In parts of Lambeth those selling drugs do so openly. It is the

norm for many of my constituents to be accosted on their way home from the Tube by dealers selling drugs. I, myself, on two occasions, walking alone in Stockwell have been offered skunk weed.

It is time the 'establishment' who have condoned this experiment sit up and listen. They need to understand the social impact it is having on already deprived and neglected communities ... The message sent out to youngsters is that taking drugs is socially acceptable. Even more dangerous is the message that taking drugs is not harmful ... It doesn't take long to see the effects on youngsters on the streets and estates. Some children are out of their heads at 9 a.m. and if they do make it to school, they are unable to learn, having lost any ambition or self-respect.

Yet a few weeks later, senior police officers were still behaving as if the change was entirely benevolent and wholly successful. The *Evening Standard* disclosed that:

Police chiefs are planning to extend the Lambeth 'softly softly' approach on cannabis across the country – despite warnings from community leaders that drugs are wrecking children's lives.

Several police forces in England and Wales will adopt the Association of Chief Police Officers and the Metropolitan Police's more relaxed attitude in which people are warned rather than arrested when caught with small amounts of the drug.

The MP for Vauxhall, Kate Hoey, voiced the concerns of many community leaders in Lambeth when she said the experiment, which effectively decriminalises cannabis, was augmenting the drug problems.

'There are more drug dealers on the streets than ever,' she said'.

In the *Mail on Sunday* of 14 June 2002, Jason Lewis reported that the Home Office had tried to muffle opposition to liberalisation among police officers. Mr Lewis wrote,

> A senior police officer asked to evaluate the controversial 'softly softly' cannabis experiment in South London was told his report was 'too negative' by Home Office officials.
>
> The extraordinary verdict shows the full extent of Home Secretary David Blunkett's determination to view the pilot scheme as a success and as a precursor for last week's reclassification of the drug.
>
> Mr Blunkett decided to downgrade cannabis to a Class C drug despite evidence of a huge increase in street robberies since the scheme in Lambeth was brought in. People in the inner-city borough were more likely to be mugged than anywhere else in Britain last year.

Government pressure, the story went on to say, had 'stifled' opposition from within the Met. Deputy Assistant Commissioner Michael Fuller, head of the Metropolitan Police's drug directorate, had delivered a very critical report to the Home Secretary. 'But, according to senior Scotland Yard sources, it was dismissed by Home Office officials. A source close to Mr Fuller said: "His analysis did not go down too well with the Home Secretary. He was told his findings were too negative." The report was shelved and never made public. Indeed, members of the Metropolitan Police Authority, whose job is to oversee the force, have never been shown a copy'.

Lewis wrote that Scotland Yard's senior management were divided on the experiment.

> It is understood Deputy Commissioner Ian Blair was virulently opposed. But within days the scheme had been revealed in the London Evening Standard and been approved to run for an initial six months by the Scotland Yard management.

The reclassification of cannabis was high on the political agenda and the success of the Lambeth scheme was seen as a key element in showing how it would work.

What had started out as an attempt to free officers from paperwork and to allow them to concentrate on serious crime, became the testing ground for new Government policy.

Soon Scotland Yard and even the officers on the beat in Lambeth found themselves under tremendous pressure to prove that the experiment was working. A questionnaire sent to all 860 officers in Brixton, was answered by only 51.

This, it was argued, showed most officers had no problems with the experiment, even though the majority of those who responded actually disagreed with it.

A Scotland Yard source said ... 'No one wanted to be the person to tell the Government the scheme did not work'.

And so the Brixton pilot scheme was officially classified a success, the ACPO circulated forces with the news, and the policy of the 'Cannabis Warning' was quietly introduced. The repeated use of the phrase 'softly, softly', to describe the police's retreat from the law, is of course the first part of an old saying, 'Softly, softly, catchee monkey'. But in this case, the monkey is not caught, and catching him is not the intention. If he were caught he would be given a caution and set free. The only thing that is soft is the law enforcement.

It is impossible to say how many cannabis offences the police now actually ignore, because they know that there is nothing to be gained in pursuing them. Once again, the endlessly flexible 1971 Act had survived officially unamended. But in fact the slow, incremental implementation of the Wootton Report was now almost complete. The favourite drug of the 1960s generation was now decriminalised in all but name, and those who might have opposed this change had not even noticed.

21

The great red herring – 'medical marijuana'

For many years, the cannabis campaign has suggested that this drug has serious medical uses. I have not space or time in this book to deal with this debate, which only touches on the edge of its main theme. But I thought it worthwhile to point out that orthodoxy on this, as on so many other parts of the debate, is more open to dispute than many people think.

There is no doubt that cannabis can, by its intoxicating effects, give sufferers from various diseases the impression that their symptoms are being relieved.

There are several difficulties with these claims. Often they are not objectively measurable. It is hard to test them against placebos, as it is impossible to take cannabis in any effective quantity without knowing that you have taken it. Cannabis's far-from-complete safety record makes it a dangerous choice of drug for anyone. Its powers of intoxication outweigh its alleged benefits. In many cases – such as the treatment of glaucoma – there are alternative drugs which experts in the disease say are superior.

Having met and debated with several people who assert that 'medical marijuana' has been useful to them, I would ask why such people so readily ally themselves to campaigns for the general decriminalisation of the drug. For it is as supporters of such campaigns that I have always met them.

They would get much further, much faster (assuming their claims are true) if they stood aside from such campaigns, which raise much wider questions. Why, if your principal concern is urgent relief of pain or other symptoms, sacrifice a possible victory on a very narrow front, for the distant possibility of total decriminalisation? If you truly believe that cannabis is a medical wonder drug, then it would surely be sensible to campaign for it to be licensed specifically and narrowly, as is medical morphine. The last thing you would need would be the support of a crowd of red-eyed, maundering hippy veterans seeking a pot-fuelled paradise.

Either these people are being unconsciously used, or they are conscious propagandists for the cause of cannabis legalisation. Certainly, the effect of the 'medical cannabis' argument has been to assist the general legalisation argument, rather than to establish THC as a recognised medicine.

But I have one further point. In an unguarded moment, one of the most prominent and skilful campaigners for cannabis legalisation, Keith Stroup, revealed many years ago what his movement really thinks about the case for 'medical cannabis'. It sees it as a red herring to get the drug a good name.

Mr Stroup, who has since claimed he has been misrepresented, is not and was not a casual amateur. He is a lawyer, and was at that time the leading figure in NORML, the National Organisation for the Reform of Marijuana Laws in the USA, founded by him in 1970. In an interview with the *Emory Wheel*[1] on 6 February 1979, Mr Stroup was

---

[1] An American university newspaper.

asked: 'How is NORML utilizing the issue of marijuana treatment of chemotherapy patients?' He replied:

> We are trying to get marijuana reclassified medically. If we do that (we'll do it in at least 20 states this year for chemotherapy patients) will be using the issue as a red herring to give marijuana a good name. That's our way of getting to them (new right) indirectly, just like the paraphernalia laws are their way at getting to us.

After the first set of brackets there appears to be a word missing. This is not my omission, but a faithful copy of the original I have before me. But I cannot think of any word apart from 'we' which could or would fill the gap. It might equally well be a botched transcription of 'we'll'.

The 'medical cannabis' campaign, as Mr Stroup memorably told us, is a conscious red herring. No serious drug could be administered in the forms in which cannabis is taken by almost all of those who use it for pleasure. There are now, on both sides of the Atlantic, properly measurable drugs made from THC, and the recent introduction of Sativex in the United Kingdom is an important success for the 'medical cannabis' lobby. It plainly requires deep and detailed research.[2]

Mr Stroup plainly accepts that these words do not help his cause. In fact they are extremely damaging to it. That is presumably why he has made strenuous efforts to suggest that he was misrepresented. He wrote, on this subject, to a Mr Steve Kubby, on 28 May 2001:

> I received a note ... telling me you were engaged yesterday in a debate in which your opponent was (once again) claiming falsely

---

[2] This author is currently examining the matter, but a complete investigation would delay the publication of this book.

that I had said in a debate in 1973 that we (NORML) were using the medical use issue as a 'red herring' for legalization. That is obviously a lie, and it suggests how desperate these drug warriors have become ... if they were really interested in my views on the medical use issue, they would ask me, rather than come up with some sound bite from a speech I gave nearly 30 years ago and try to twist the meaning into something that suits their political agenda.

Alas for this explanation, the words were not said (as Mr Stroup mistakenly says) in a speech, nor were they said in 1973. They were spoken in an interview with the *Wheel*, described as having been given in a 'post-debate encounter' on 26 January 1979.

Mr Stroup says later in the letter that 'I might well have said that the medical use issue was a "red herring", because it diverts attention away from the larger issue'.

This is not the case at all. The Emory University library still holds a file of the magazine. I have obtained a copy to see what it actually contains. Mr Stroup was free to check the record as I did. The interviewers are not hostile to Mr Stroup, or trying to trip him up.

The question runs (note its wording): 'How is NORML utilizing the issue of marijuana treatment of chemotherapy patients?' In answer, Mr Stroup makes no attempt to deny that NORML is 'utilizing' the issue, or to suggest that the choice of words is wrong. On the contrary, he entirely accepts this formulation. He couldn't have accepted it had he thought – as he suggests he did in the letter to Mr Kubby – that the medical issue was a red herring 'because it diverts attention away from the larger issue'.

Mr Stroup's letter says of his campaigning work that,

> it was not until 1972 that we became aware of the possible medical uses of marijuana, and petitioned the federal government to

reclassify marijuana to permit physicians to prescribe it when appropriate ... we considered the question of decriminalizing or legalizing marijuana for recreational use to be the principal issue, as it involved tens of millions of Americans, hundreds of thousands of whom were being arrested each year.

I might well have said that the medical use issue was a 'red herring', because it diverts attention away from the larger issue. Our opponents are now suggesting that we were trying to use the medical issue to lure people unsuspectingly to our larger agenda, when the opposite was true.

He incidentally explains why the 'medical marijuana' issue has been and remains such an effective campaign tool. Many more people are prepared to support moves to weaken the law when this argument is used:

At NORML we have always been forthright about our support for legalizing both medical use and recreational use, and we have always said that each issue must be considered and evaluated on its own merits. Right now, 3 out of 4 Americans support the medical use of marijuana, while the country is about evenly divided over the recreational issue.

It is certainly the case that a steadily growing number of the states in the USA (and the District of Columbia) have now adopted 'medical marijuana' laws in one form or another, which have effectively legalised the sale of quite large quantities of cannabis. Likewise, there is no doubt that the growing British public acceptance of decriminalisation is boosted greatly by a widespread belief in the 'medical cannabis' case. It was, for instance, referred to sympathetically by the Runciman (Police Foundation) Report in 2000. A discussion of its alleged medical uses forms a large part of *The Science of*

Marijuana,[3] a book by Professor Leslie Iversen, a leading figure in the British government's drugs establishment. Professor Iversen, who is not among the conservatives in the argument about drug laws, wrote 'There are clearly several possible therapeutic indications for cannabis-based medicines, but for most of them evidence for the clinical effectiveness of the drug is woefully inadequate by modern standards'.[4]

He argues that it is possible to amass reliable evidence, citing studies in the treatment of sickness caused by cancer chemotherapy. But he adds 'One of the obvious complications in the medical use of cannabis is that the window between its therapeutic effects and the cannabis-induced high is often narrow'.[5]

This caution, coming from such a source, underlines the problem. How can we objectively distinguish between the euphoria of the drug, and its effects on the perception of symptoms, and its actual operation on the diseases it is supposed to treat?

Perhaps those who have credulously accepted this argument might at least consider the possibility that Mr Stroup was telling the truth all those years ago, and they have in fact been misled by a very clever red herring. It may well be that cannabis, or its active ingredients, has serious medical uses. It seems to me to be far too soon to be definitive on the matter. But if it does, these uses will not be connected with its power to intoxicate, and will have to be balanced very carefully against the growing worries that it is a risk to mental health.

The conduct, and the effect, of the medical marijuana campaign have without doubt made this drug more easily available to healthy people in the USA, and strengthened the campaign for its general

---

[3] Oxford University Press, 2000.
[4] *The Science of Marijuana*, p.174.
[5] pp.174–5.

decriminalisation in Britain. These facts tend to support the assertion that medical marijuana is a 'red herring' to 'give marijuana a good name'. After all, the person who said so was and remains one of the leading campaigners against the cannabis laws. And the medical marijuana campaign has never distanced itself from the general campaign for looser legislation, something it would surely have done had it believed the case was urgent and necessary.

22

Freeing up or freeing down?

Study almost any argument for relaxing the cannabis laws, especially those advanced by the police, and you will find at some point the claim that spending less time on the pursuit of cannabis will 'free up' the police to 'crack down' on the real problem. This problem is stated or implied to be the supposedly 'harder' drugs, such as heroin and cocaine, and of course the 'evil dealers' who press these on their innocent, addicted or otherwise pitiable victims, the users.

During 2011, I struggled with the press offices of the Home Office and the Department of Justice to obtain two sets of figures. I sought details of arrests for possession or trafficking of Class 'A' drugs. And then I sought figures on how such offenders had been disposed of by the courts.

At the time of writing, my efforts have met with small success. Apparently the official statistics are not broken down in such a way as to reveal this information in any detail.

However, Nicola Blackwood, the MP for Oxford West and Abingdon, did manage to obtain the following figures through a series of Parliamentary questions, in co-operation with Tim Knox and Kathy Gyngell of the Centre for Policy Studies. They refer (as do most of my figures) to England and Wales alone.[1]

They showed that during 2010, 2,530 people were convicted and sentenced for supply of 'Class A' drugs. Of these, 1,756 did not even go to prison and none received the maximum sentence (the so-called 'life' tariff, which is of course nothing of the kind).

They contain comparative tables for what happened to those convicted of drug offences, in the years 2007–2010. They do not vary all that much, year to year, so I have extracted some facts from the most recent table, that for 2010. This shows that for 'Class A', drugs supposedly the most serious, 12,175 people were sentenced for simple possession in 2010.

Of these, only 779 – fewer than one in ten – were sent to prison. There is no information in the answer on which I can base even a guess as to why these were selected for imprisonment and the rest not, though one might suspect (especially after reading the account of Peter Doherty's treatment below) that a long previous record, a combination of this offence with other crimes, or a very large quantity possessed, might make a difference.

Of those imprisoned, just two, repeat two, received the maximum sentence of seven years (three years, six months would be served, in practice, and quite possibly less). The others, 11,396, received 'other sentences'.

It seems likely that most were, in effect, let off provided they agreed to undergo some sort of 'rehabilitation' programme, quite possibly involving methadone prescriptions. The figures give no idea as to how many of these were first offenders, or serial offenders.

---

[1] The figures can be found in *Hansard*, House of Commons, 15 June 2011, c839W. The Minister answering is Crispin Blunt.

Even for *supply* of Class 'A' drugs (supposedly so serious that the maximum sentence is 'life' in prison, which of course doesn't mean anything of the kind), 774 out of 2, 530 convicted offenders did not go to prison at all, let alone for life. For the similar offence of 'Possession with Intent to Supply', the figures are higher but the proportions are similar: 3687 sentenced, 908 imprisoned, one for life.

And, if the relaxation of cannabis law enforcement has 'freed up' police and courts for pursuing the 'evil dealers', why have convictions for supply of Class 'A' drugs remained more or less unchanged for the past four years (2,633 in 2007, 2,968 in 2008, 2,804 in 2009 and 2,530 in 2010)?

It seems highly unlikely, especially given the enormous consumption of cocaine in modern Britain, that these figures bear any relation even to the numbers of dealers in operation, let alone to the numbers of users.

Under these circumstances, I think it is instructive to mention two cases of prominent people caught in possession of Class 'A' drugs, to see how they were dealt with.

One of the most striking is the alleged singer Peter Doherty, who has repeatedly been brought to court for drugs offences. On 21 December 2009, Doherty appeared at Gloucester Crown Court to be sentenced for driving and drugs offences committed the previous June. The officers who stopped him found one 'wrap' of heroin in the car, worth up to £35, and what was described as a 'homemade crack pipe on the driver's seat'. A search of Doherty's country home had uncovered a further 15 'wraps' worth around £350. Doherty admitted to two counts of drugs possession, driving without a licence and without insurance. At that stage Doherty had 21 previous drug offences to his name. He was fined a total of £2,050 for the drugs and traffic offences.

As he left the court, yet another 'wrap' of heroin was seen by a security guard to fall from his coat pocket (actual police officers nowadays rarely patrol court buildings).

He was not held in custody. But he was charged and tried for the offence a few weeks later, on 26 January, this time at Gloucester Magistrates Court. That day, Doherty walked free once again – fined £750, with £85 costs. The Judge passed this sentence after being told that Doherty (who had arrived late for his trial, blaming his satellite navigation) was not 'mickey taking' and had simply forgotten the drugs were in one of his many coats.

District Judge Joti Boparai then ruled that, as Doherty was paying for drug 'treatment' privately, it would not be worth using public money to put him on a 'rehabilitation' order. Prison does not seem to have been considered.

Judge Boparai said: 'Either this was sheer stupidity or a ploy to get more publicity'.

Whatever the truth, there is no doubt that it demonstrated two things. One, that drug offenders in modern Britain are not afraid of the law, and two, that they are right not to be afraid.

A fascinating picture of the state of English criminal justice is given in the newspaper accounts of the trial.

The Prosecutor, Malcolm Hayes, said the new charge was due to the vigilance of a security guard, Richard Dando, who had seen the packages – worth £192 – fall to the floor.

Mr Hayes said: 'He (Doherty) said he felt stupid that it did indeed drop from his pocket'.

The case was discussed almost entirely as if it had been a mishap or wardrobe malfunction, rather than the detection of a crime. His possession of large quantities of an illegal drug supposedly regarded with special horror by the law was almost incidental to the case, which was dealt with as little more than a silly misfortune.

Apparently Doherty's large wardrobe was mainly to blame. He may not even have chosen his own clothes. His defence lawyer, Bruce Clark, explained:

He has a great many items of clothing – suits and clothes going into the hundreds. There were residual drugs which he had left in one coat pocket. He didn't necessarily choose the coat for himself.

He has a large number of suits and indicated that he had previously found lumps the size of his fist in his pockets, and had forgotten these items were there.

Mr Clark continued: 'He is a recovering heroin addict and has received some very sophisticated medical treatment. He had been an addict for some years and is a very well known, famous musician with a huge international reputation'.

The whole case seemed to be concerned with Doherty's excuses for bringing his illegal drugs into the court buildings, entirely ignoring (or seeing as normal) the actual offence – committed by a person with a very long record of drugs convictions – of possessing an illegal Class 'A' drug at all. Certainly there is no evidence that the police or the law look especially sternly on the drug, or are interested in how and where Doherty obtained it.

The Judge at one stage mused 'You could have thought he would have checked what he was wearing'.

This is certainly true, but it is surely of no interest to a Judge in a criminal case, to wonder why the defendant is so stupid as to bring an illegal substance (supposedly one specially frowned on by the law) into a criminal court, and there drop it on the floor in sight of a court official. The issue before him was the undoubted guilt of Doherty, and its exacerbation by the act of flaunting the crime in a criminal court building. Yet even under these circumstances, and even with his long record of drug offences, Doherty was not imprisoned.

Mr Clark said: 'He was coming in a hurry. He was very embarrassed and felt very stupid because of it. He has a great responsibility in relation to promotion and to people he works with'.

The general excuse-making of 'rehabilitation' and 'harm-reduction', which treat wilful drug abuse as a pitiable disease, depriving its sufferers of their wills, were of course deployed. Doherty was said to be using medical implants which cancelled out the effect of heroin. His lawyer went to far as to state 'It's working for him'. The judge, who seemed familiar with Doherty, even remarked, 'He does look better in physical appearance. Last time I saw him he was sweating quite profusely'.

Another curious case at about this time was widely seen as special treatment for the rich and famous. But was it really?

On 15 July 2008, shortly after Doherty's arrest for traffic and drugs offences, two very rich people were charged with possessing crack cocaine and heroin. Hans Kristian Rausing and his wife Eva, heirs to the gigantic TetraPak fortune, were arrested after Mrs Rausing tried to smuggle the drugs into the American Embassy in London. Police who searched the Rausings' home discovered more drugs. Both were charged and released on bail. But on 29 July all the charges against them were officially dropped at the Westminster magistrates' court, The pair were ordered instead to go to Charing Cross police station where they were 'cautioned'.[2]

Newspaper reports suggested that police had originally wanted to 'caution' the couple because of the 'small amount' of drugs found on them, deemed to be for personal use, and because it was their first offence.

But the Crown Prosecution Service duty lawyer is said to have decided to charge them. He seems to have been overruled. The result was a curious procedure known as a 'conditional caution'.

On 30 July, Neil Sears wrote in the *Daily Mail* that the maximum sentence for possession of Class A drugs was seven years in prison.

---

[2] Mrs Rausing was found dead in distressing circumstances in July 2012.

And 'those convicted of possession with intent to supply – charges which can apply even to those providing only their own friends and relatives with drugs with no intention of making any profit – can be jailed for life'.

But he added:

> The sentences sound tough, *but in practice the maximum penalties are almost never imposed* (my italics).
>
> And as drug consumption has soared, taking Britain to near the top of the European table for cocaine abuse, *there has been a huge growth in the use of cautions instead of full prosecutions leading to conviction* (my italics).
>
> Labour's downgrading of cannabis has led to a fall in prosecutions over possession of that drug, but those caught with small amounts of cocaine also have a good chance of escaping with a caution.

There was then much fuss about the rich being better treated than others, and about the Rausing family's large donations to the Conservative Party. However, little evidence was produced that others caught in possession of cocaine were suffering heavy sentences.

The report noted that the then Metropolitan Police Commissioner, Sir Ian Blair, had attracted some attention by proclaiming that middle-class addicts who snort cocaine at dinner parties were not above the law. His bluster had, as so often, borne little relation to reality and he had been badly embarrassed by the reality of the Rausing case. Other celebrities, the newspapers reported, had also been let off lightly. But did this show that the rich and famous were being treated leniently? Or was it the case that these were the only cases which caught the public attention, and that, in general, possession of the bogeyman drugs was not being dealt with by severe punishment? I have, at the time of writing, been unable to obtain official figures.

But we should note, from the same period as the Rausing case, the following celebrity drug episodes:

- No action was taken to prosecute the prominent model Kate Moss despite the publication of images of her apparently snorting white powder.
- George Michael, the singer, was arrested in a public lavatory in possession of cocaine and cannabis. He was reported to have told police that his charity work would suffer if he was charged (a drugs conviction would have stopped him going to the USA for an AIDS fund-raising concert). He said he was sorry, the police decided not to refer the case to Crown Prosecution Service and he was freed with – a 'caution'.

The Homosexual Rights Campaigner Peter Tatchell wrote at the time:

> You may find it surprising coming from me, as I have often defended George Michael and his sexuality. But enough is enough. He is now just the latest big-name celebrity caught in possession of hard drugs to get away with a gentle ticking off. In fact, it seems to happen a lot of the time.

Tatchell complained that 'laughable footage of the singer Amy Winehouse (whose own father has said he wishes she could be locked up to prevent her killing herself with drugs) with what appeared to be crack, proved insufficient for police to charge her'. The complaint seems especially poignant now that Miss Winehouse is dead after her short and excessive life. Defenders of illegal drugs have correctly pointed out that the direct cause of Amy Winehouse's death appears to have been legal alcohol. But this raises an interesting question. Is it possible that the increasing use of alcohol by the young, in devastating quantities, is at least partly caused by the common use of other (illegal) drugs whose sole purpose is self-stupefaction?

23

Some notes on harm reduction and rehabilitation

The aim of this book is to show definitively that the principal argument of Britain's drugs lobby is false through and through. There is no war on drugs in this country, and there has not been such a war for many decades. There is no 'prohibition' or anything resembling it. Whatever may have caused our current drug problems, excessive conservative persecution of drug users did not do so.

It is tempting to explore several side effects of this falsehood, but, were I to do so, I doubt I should ever come to the end.

I would just note that two features of modern Britain are connected to the unacknowledged drugs policy of Her Majesty's Government – a policy of accepting the sale and use of technically illegal drugs in practice, especially of cannabis, but also of heroin and cocaine.

One of these is the almost universally accepted concept of 'rehabilitation'. This requires convicted or arrested drug users (though not those caught with cannabis, to whom nothing happens at all in most cases) to undergo various programmes supposedly aimed at weaning them off the drugs they have been taking. In return for entering these programmes, the abusers are frequently spared fines or imprisonment.

I shall not seek to argue here about the rightness or wrongness of this concept. I will examine it on its own terms. And first, I would point out that it directly contradicts the normal idea of law and justice.

Consider. The drug involved (heroin or cocaine) is so illegal that in some cases a supplier of it can be sent to prison for 'life', which is certainly several years. He may also face confiscation of his wealth under autocratic and dubious new powers obtained from Parliament for this specific purpose. Possessing it is also illegal – and in the cases of heroin and cocaine it is still technically possible to be sent to prison for this offence.

Thus the act of possessing it is a wilful crime. This crime could not have come about if someone else had not committed the wilful crimes of importation and sale.

These laws can only really be justified if the state recognises its right to intervene in such matters, in defiance of the views of the *Economist* and the alleged opinions on the subject of John Stuart Mill. It may appear to do so. But does it? Apart from occasional rhetoric about 'evil drug dealers',[1] it is now rare to hear any attempts, informed or not, to justify the law's interference. It also appears that the law is feebler than it appears, in practical operation.

The whole theory of 'rehabilitation' is in fact a direct contradiction of the idea that the law should punish possession of these drugs. To deter addiction, you would have to punish the offence of possession from the first. But you cannot simultaneously punish and 'rehabilitate'. One action is based on the principle that the action is wrong, cannot be permitted and should be dealt with by an exemplary penalty which

---

[1] See the Conservative Party Manifesto of 2002.

is unpleasant to the convicted person, and spreads fear among those who might be considering the same offence. The other is based upon assuming that the individual's drug use is a cry for help, and that it must therefore be a reason for sympathy. Further, 'rehabilitation', which generally takes the form of replacing the illegal drug with a legal substitute, or of a slow and sometimes interminable process of 'weaning off', involves the state in helping the convicted person do the very thing for which he has been convicted, or something so similar that it is very hard to tell the difference.

The idea of 'addiction' is widely accepted by courts and legislators, and also generally accepted in society as a whole. Setting aside any debate on the validity of this rather circular concept, and accepting – for the sake of argument – that the repeated use of 'addictive' drugs really does rob the user of his or her will, what are we left with for the law to do?

The answer seems quite straightforward. If this is the case, and use of the drug leads swiftly to addiction, then the law has one opportunity to save the individual from 'addiction' – by deterring him from taking the drug in the first place. He is not going to catch 'addiction', like a cold. To become 'addicted', he is going to have find people who are ready to supply the drug to him, and he will then need to decide to take quite radical steps to pierce his own skin and pump it into his bloodstream. Let us, once again for the sake of argument, assume that one such episode will rob him of his will thereafter, and make him a helpless victim of the drug's 'addictive' power. If we accept that once he is 'addicted' he is likely to become a menace to his family and his neighbours, then we are justified in using deterrent punishment to persuade the undecided not to risk 'addiction'.

Deterrent punishment is not principally aimed at the person punished, though it may help him give up his criminal habits. It is there to discourage the others, who are considering committing the crime involved. So logically, if we genuinely believe in 'addiction', think it a bad thing and so wish to reduce it, we should severely punish – from the first offence – the individuals who are found in possession of illegal 'addictive' drugs.

Implied in this discussion is a recognition that taking such drugs is actually enjoyable, and that drug takers ingest drugs for pleasure, and ignore warnings against them because they enjoy taking them so much. But this blazing truth cannot be mentioned. The idea that people take drugs for selfish pleasure, rather than because they are victims of something or other, cannot coexist with our present policy, which is based on the idea that drug 'addicts' are the victims of 'evil dealers', who cunningly persuade them into unwanted lives of irresistible 'addiction'. It also contradicts the widespread belief that 'addicts' have turned to drugs out of misfortune, poverty, 'deprivation' or abuse. A telling example of this is a letter written in February 1999 by Somerset police to Rebecca Trebble, who reported that her car had been vandalised. Superintendent John Snell responded,

> Whilst I have every sympathy with you being a victim of crime, the position regarding victims is not limited to those who suffer as you have done.
>
> Many of those who are responsible for the commission of such minor crimes could be considered to be victims themselves. To my knowledge some of our prolific offenders are heroin addicts who live in the very worst of housing conditions in our area in relative poverty. It is also true many of them are from broken homes and really have miserable family backgrounds.

This is not an unfair summary of the general attitude of the British criminal justice system in the twenty-first century. It is interesting to see that the sociological indoctrination of the police has gone so far that a Superintendent in a rural county is familiar with the useful (in this case) concept of 'relative poverty'.

While the 'evil dealers' can be punished with deterrent sentences, their customers (who in the eyes of authority are also their victims) must be helped, through rehabilitation. I explored this strange contradiction, under which the evil nature of a drug vanishes once it is actually being consumed for its intended purpose, in my introductory chapter.

But actually the British authorities are severely inconsistent, if they truly believe in the menace of 'addiction'. Far from imposing severe deterrent penalties on those found in possession of 'addictive' drugs, they indulge them with repeated opportunities for 'rehabilitation' or 'treatment' (as provided to Peter Doherty, for example). This policy means there is no serious deterrent in law to the action which leads to 'addiction'.

If 'addiction' is so inescapable once it has been contracted, then surely great efforts should be made to prevent it in the first place? Yet nothing of the sort happens. The authorities simply do not operate in accordance with their supposed beliefs. The existing system, if not actively designed to encourage people to take up illegal drugs, treats them from the very start with so much sympathy and indulgence that they can reasonably conclude that authority does not disapprove of what they are doing. So they become 'addicts'.

Later, the authorities become the drug abusers' actual supplier, often providing drugs free of charge.

This, in many cases is the form that 'rehabilitation' and 'treatment' take.

There are believed to be 220,000 drug users undergoing 'treatment' in the United Kingdom.[2] Professor Neil McKeganey, of Glasgow

---

[2] *Controversies in Drugs, policy and practice*, Neil McKeganey, Palgrave Macmillan 2011, p.63.

University, estimates that £900 million is being spent each year on such 'treatment'.[3] He argues that much of it is poorly managed, poorly monitored and is handled by poorly qualified individuals with low levels of expertise.

Above all, a very large part of it consists of the methadone programme, by which users of (illegal) heroin are supplied, at taxpayers' expense, with a (legal) substitute with effects very similar to those of heroin itself. Professor McKeganey argues[4] that the most effective treatment methods – residential rehabilitation centres – are those which are least often provided.

He estimates that in Scotland alone the methadone programme may be costing £40 million a year (the United Kingdom figure is estimated at £300 million), but reckons that in Scotland it is enabling fewer than 5 per cent of addicts to become drug free.[5] And he says that in Edinburgh, there are now more deaths associated with methadone use than with heroin use.[6]

McKeganey also points out a simple truth about the 'safe injecting centres' so strongly favoured by the 'harm reduction' movement, and often preached as some sort of solution to the heroin problem. His argument is obvious, but rarely stated: 'just as with needle and syringe exchange, safe injecting centres may have the unintended consequence of further entrenching a risky form of drug use – resulting in the individual persisting with injecting for longer than they otherwise might have done'.[7]

This is putting it mildly. By offering these services, the state itself becomes a drug supplier, extorting money from taxpayers with the

---

[3] p.66.
[4] p.64.
[5] (*Controversies*, p.64).
[6] p.33.
[7] p.37.

force of law, to finance a socially damaging habit, all but indistinguishable from the criminal consumption of illegal heroin. It also facilitates the habit, and endorses it, by providing the paraphernalia by which the supposedly illegal drug is pumped into the bodies of its illegal users. The confusion is endless. One has to ask why the government does not mount a campaign against itself, as the principal 'Evil Drug Dealer' in the country. But of course it does not truly regard the drugs as evil, and its rhetorical militancy towards the dealers is a cover for its actual complaisance towards the users.

In Her Majesty's Prisons, which contain people sentenced for the supply of heroin, notices to visitors contradictorily preach the virtues of needle exchange. This procedure, while powerfully undermining the anti-drugs message of the law, does not even work. McKeganey points out[8] that the Unlinked Anonymous Surveillance Programme recorded a mere 1 per cent drop in dangerous needle-sharing between 1991 and 2006 (from 24 per cent of injectors to 23 per cent), despite the distribution in the intervening 15 years of millions of needles and syringes at public expense.

In the prisons themselves, supposedly more under the control of the law than anywhere else in the country, a 2003 survey showed that 30 per cent of prisoners had used cannabis within prison at least weekly; 16 per cent had used cocaine, 11 per cent had used crack and 36 per cent had used heroin.[9]

This is combined with government propaganda, such as the official 'Talk to Frank' site, which adopt a jokey and amoral consumer guide attitude towards drug taking, and appear to assume

---

[8] p.40.
[9] Bullock, T. 'Changing levels of drug use before during and after imprisonment', in M. Ramsay (editor) 'Prisoners' Drug Use and Treatment: Seven Studies'. Home Office research study 267).

that it is going to take place anyway. Funds for this 'harm reduction' approach are readily available. Groups such as the National Drug Prevention Alliance, which urges abstinence from drugs and stresses their illegality, are poorly supported and so have limited impact. The pioneering work of former teacher Mary Brett on the damaging effects of cannabis on schoolchildren, and her potent and proven anti-drug material for use in schools, struggles to obtain distribution.

As Professor McKeganey concludes[10] this is fundamentally a moral question, about what sort of society we wish to have. He points out 'The principle of pragmatism has been so influential within the drugs sphere that it has become almost a term of abuse to suggest that someone's view of illegal drug use is rooted in a moral view of the world'.

But why has that principle been so overpoweringly dominant? In a final chapter, I will study the 2002 report into drugs of the House of Commons Home Affairs Committee, a body which – significantly – included our current prime minister.

This document provided a clear exposition of the prevailing attitude of official and political Britain to the drug problem. As I write, a successor committee is making a new investigation which I can only hope is less dominated by amoral pragmatism, defeat and self-deception. But even if it is, it will have to work very hard to undo the damage done by its forerunner.

---

[10] p.165.

24

The demoralisation of Britain

The greatest success of the drug decriminalisation campaign has, from the start, been its respectability. Though it is true that a handful of open revolutionaries put their names to the 1967 cannabis manifesto, they were overshadowed by the long lists of the grand, the famous and the established. Most people, when they see a former editor of *The Times* or a former Defence Secretary or a distinguished doctor endorsing weaker drug laws, think this means that sensible, responsible, conservative people have come round to this view.

It is my contention that it shows something quite different – that a formerly conservative establishment has been demoralised – a possibility I explored in *The Abolition of Britain*.

Readers of this history will have to make up their own minds which view they accept. One problem for anyone dealing with this subject is the strange fate of the British Conservative Party, which, having for some years believed in nothing at all, then embraced fervent economic liberalism under Margaret Thatcher. Economic liberalism is of course closely allied to political and social liberalism, and Lady Thatcher's government, whether it meant to or not, pursued or at the very least did not thwart these forces. But millions of people, some Lady Thatcher's worshippers and some of them filled with unshakeable loathing of her, have fallen into the mistake of believing that her years in power – because they were certainly not socialist – were therefore 'right-wing' and ultra-conservative.

I have tried to explain why this is not so in *The Cameron Delusion* and will not do so again here. Let it only be said that there is a coherent conservative critique of the Thatcher government, conservative in the sense of social, cultural and moral matters, as well as in the area of national sovereignty and human liberty. There is also a conservative critique of the British Labour Party which, having abandoned its old beliefs in trade unionism and state control of the economy for the betterment of the working class, has become the political arm of the new class of urban graduates who wish above all to be liberated from the narrow moral confines of the suburbs, and the Protestant restraints of British Puritanism.

I would argue that the conservative is compelled to reject the idea of self-stupefaction as wrong in itself. And he is also compelled to accept that, if stupefying drugs are widely available, that it is permissible to use the law to deter their use. The economic and social liberal, however, tends to take the view of the *Economist*, and the supposed view of John Stuart Mill, that the individual is sovereign. The New Labour radical, for slightly different reasons, takes the same position. But because the Labour Party (after long years of fellow-travelling with pro-Soviet Communists) still fears the mistrust of respectable voters, it is often Conservative politicians who feel confident to go the furthest down this track. The behaviour of the Tory Shadow Cabinet towards Ann Widdecombe's proposals for a minor revival of punishment for cannabis is an example of this. While eccentric individuals in the Labour Party might take the same view, notably Marjorie Mowlam, Labour's high command continued to *appear* resolute against liberalisation.

So it was that in summer of 2001, the former Tory Cabinet Minister Peter Lilley, aided by a think tank, the Social Market Foundation, published a foolish pamphlet about drugs, which won him much acclaim. It was called 'Common Sense on Cannabis: The Conservative Case for Change'.

Its 'arguments' are wearily familiar. First is defeatism, mixed with an admission that in fact the law is not enforced. Next is its determination to fail to see any connection between its non-enforcement and its failure. Mr Lilley argued 'The decriminalisation of cannabis is inevitable. Indeed, it is happening already. In many parts of the country the police no longer prosecute cannabis users'.

This interesting fact is left unexplained and unexplored. To do so would be a nuisance, so on we stride, proclaiming 'The problem is not simply that the current law is unenforceable – it is also indefensible'. No evidence is produced for it being unenforce*able*, though it is certainly unenforced. But never mind. Mr Lilley presses on with a case that will perhaps make him popular among *Guardian* readers: 'The arguments for criminalisation of cannabis that we hear so often crumble on analysis. Laws that can neither be enforced nor defended cannot survive. The issue is no longer whether the law should be changed but how'.

But what is the evidence that they *cannot* be enforced, as he repeatedly claims? None is produced, though there is plenty that they *are not* being enforced. Following another spasm of defeatism, he continued with these curious suggestions. First, 'Those of a conservative disposition could and should make a tactical withdrawal to a much more defensible position which states that removal of legal penalties does not imply public approval of cannabis use, still less of abuse'.

This is the opposite of the truth. The only reason for the existence of a law of this kind is a moral disapproval of the drug's effects on those who use it. If it does not embody and express such a disapproval, then what is or was its purpose?

In a society such as modern Britain, with weak morals, the law must play a greater part than conservatives might like. But that is an argument for strengthening morality, not for weakening the law.

Mr Lilley continues,

> Rather, it is for the individual to exercise personal responsibility in the use of cannabis as of alcohol. And it is for parents, teachers and pastors to teach what is right in this area, not for the law, or for politicians to curtail our freedom to act responsibly.

At a time when it was increasingly clear that – following the abolition of the 1915 alcohol licensing laws – moral restraints on alcohol abuse in Britain were fast breaking down, this was hardly a strong argument. The weakening of the law had not been countered or moderated by any moral force. The opposite had happened. Freedom to act responsibly is granted to those who are able and willing to act responsibly. Far from there being evidence that legal restraints, once withdrawn, would be replaced by moral restraints, there was by 2001 plenty of evidence of the reverse. When the legal restraints were withdrawn, there was no restraint left at all.

Mr Lilley then falls into the trap of accepting the non-existent and unscientific distinction between 'hard' and 'soft' drugs:

> Above all we should recognise that penalisation of cannabis use, far from preventing people sliding down a slippery slope from soft drugs to hard drugs, actually makes that descent more likely. This is because it brings the soft drug user into contact with the hard drug pusher since both types of drug are forced through the same illegal channels. The most important objective of changing the law on cannabis must be to break this link.

Mr Lilley then pleads: 'I simply want to prevent the demonisation of cannabis use from undermining respect for the law and traditional moral values and to protect people from exposure to criminality and hard drugs'.

This argument turns logic upside down. If a law is not being enforced (as Mr Lilley clearly admits is the case above) then it is the failure to enforce it that brings it into disrepute. The interesting question must be why it is not being enforced, and whether it could be better enforced in future. Anyway, purchasing and possessing cannabis is a crime. Those who do it are by definition criminals. It does not 'bring them into contact with criminality' as innocent persons who would otherwise have nothing to do with such a milieu. They have decided to cross the line of the law. They are already in contact with crime.

As for the 'demonisation' of cannabis, this is once again the reverse of the truth. Far from being 'demonised', the drug has been sanitised, even beatified – by being officially classified and referred to as 'soft' and also by a lengthy and well-co-ordinated public relations campaign, including Mr Keith Stroup's use of the 'medical marijuana' argument as a 'red herring' to get pot a good name. Mr Lilley seems unaware of, or complacent about, the growing correlation between this drug and mental illness.

He then announces,

> I also believe that individual freedom is threatened if the state is seen as the prime source of moral values and the sole enforcer of moral behaviour. The more people are free to exercise responsibility for their own lives, the more responsibly they are likely to lead them.

This would be true in a society of strong independent morality. But the most profound threat to freedom arises from the British people's increasing determination – led by a libertine and selfish middle class – to throw off self-restraint in their personal behaviour. Any follower of Edmund Burke knows that such behaviour forges terrible chains for the future.

We then proceed into the same logical jungle traversed by Dame Ruth. Above all, there is the misleading plaint about the supposed severity of the laws against cannabis (I have italicised those points where it is clear Mr Lilley is failing to distinguish properly between theory and practice):

> Possession for own use *can* carry a *potential* punishment of up to five years and/or a fine *if tried in a Crown Court*. More typically such offences are dealt with by a Magistrates Court in which the *maximum sentence* would be three months or a £2,500 fine or both.

Few such cases ever reach a Crown Court. Maximum sentences are rarely if ever imposed by Magistrates or anyone else. In my discussion of Ruth Runciman's report I provide figures for the disposals of such cases in reality, which make it plain that even at this stage fines of £2,500, prison terms of five years or even three months were extremely rare. Why did Mr Lilley portray matters in this way? He has been a Cabinet Minister, and knows better.

Immediately following this passage is the misleading listing of the number of arrests, without any attempt to explain properly what happens (or more important what does *not* happen) to those arrested:

> These penalties have not prevented widespread use of cannabis with the result that increasing numbers of people have fallen foul of the drugs laws. The number of people arrested for offences involving cannabis nearly quadrupled from 26,000 to 97,000 in the ten-year period from 1988 to 1998.

This statement that 'these penalties have not prevented widespread use of cannabis' is disingenuous and misleading, as we shall see shortly. The further claim that increasing numbers of people have 'fallen foul' of the drugs laws because of the failure of these penalties is equally suspect. What does he mean 'fallen foul'? Are the cannabis laws some sort of wicked, haphazard trap into which people tumble through no agency of their own? Or are they, put simply, laws which can be used to arrest and prosecute people who wilfully break them?

A man of Mr Lilley's intellect and experience has no business putting his name to this sort of thing. If the theoretical penalties he cites had in fact been consistently applied by the courts, they might well have greatly reduced (though of course not wholly prevented) the use of cannabis. We cannot know, as they were not used. But it is certainly possible – as the consistent and severe use of the law to enforce drink-driving limits, seat-belt wearing and smoking bans has repeatedly shown in the past half-century.

What is certainly misleading is to suggest that the growth in cannabis use has followed, or is in any way the result of, the imposition of such penalties. For they have not in fact been imposed.

Like Dame Ruth Runciman, Mr Lilley does not actually suppress the truth. But, by ordering his statements as he does, he avoids having to confront it directly.

Beneath this passage – and *after* Mr Lilley has produced his conclusion that the law is failing, is the only piece of information that could possibly make sense of Mr Lilley's puzzling claim that severe penalties for cannabis use have somehow led to an increase in cannabis use.

Mr Lilley states:

However, the police and the courts are enforcing the laws against cannabis with diminishing enthusiasm. As the number of arrests has grown the proportion of people let off with a caution has risen from under a third in 1988 to over half in recent years. And the proportion of those who are found guilty by the courts has declined from nearly two-thirds to under half. A survey carried out for a *Panorama* programme broadcast in November 1999 found that two-thirds of police officers would no longer prosecute someone for having a few cannabis plants. Indeed, most police officers surveyed believed cannabis to be far less harmful or addictive than alcohol or tobacco.

The recent decision by the Police Commander for Lambeth not to pursue minor cannabis offences so as to release officers to tackle more important crimes shows how de facto de-penalisation is gathering pace.

The positioning of these facts, as in the Runciman report, is highly significant. If they had been placed higher up, underneath the arrest figures and the list of severe maximum penalties, it would have been obvious that the law, as so chillingly described by Mr Lilley, was not being enforced. But as they are positioned after Mr Lilley has already reached his conclusion, they are excluded from his argument.

As is always the case in this so-called 'debate', the truth is quite obvious if you look. But nobody looks, because the truth is an argument for an option they do not want to pursue. They prefer the myth of failed 'prohibition', which has been so useful in steering Britain away from a punitive policy towards drugs without ever explicitly admitting this intention.

That is perfectly normal politics, when the elite often believes its ideas are in 'advance' of the thoughts and beliefs of the voting masses. Such cynical dishonesty, so unlovely, is common in British political action. But in this case the elite seems to have come to believe its own propaganda. This is not so much dishonesty as a kind of collective delusion. And this delusion closes the minds of the political class to a whole sphere of action.

What is the reason for this? There is the general association of drugs with radicalism which has been so important since the 1960s. But there may be another force at work. I have suggested earlier that past drug abuse, especially cannabis-smoking, is so common in the political and media classes that the most influential people in the country are prejudiced, corrupted and embarrassed by it.

The behaviour of William Hague's Shadow Cabinet is an example of this. I would add that many urban graduate professionals permit their children to use cannabis, and are worried not that it may damage them but that it may get them into trouble with the law and spoil their careers. This explains the frequent complaint that the existing law is evil because it 'criminalises' cannabis users.

An interesting insight into this sector of society was provided by the case of Brian Dodgeon, a 61-year-old university lecturer given a (suspended) eight-month prison sentence in December 2011 after several illegal drugs in the supposedly serious Class 'A' were found in his London home. The drugs were discovered by the police only after the death of a 15-year-old schoolgirl, Isobel Jones-Reilly, who had previously found and taken some of them, with fatal results.

Miss Jones-Reilly died from a drug overdose after attending a teenage party, unsupervised by adults, at Mr Dodgeon's London home. Dodgeon's 14-year-old daughter, and two 14-year-old boys, were also taken to hospital after this gathering. It is interesting to note that these events took place not in some run-down or lawless district, but in the same street where the present Education Secretary Michael Gove lives, and close to the former home of the Prime Minister, David Cameron. The teenagers had spent the evening drinking – but not only drinking – after Mr Dodgeon and his 'partner' had gone out for the night.

Around 30 teenagers attended the event, where they drank cider, wine and spirits – and smoked cannabis. Miss Jones-Reilly was known to be a regular cannabis user. Others present at the party, where cannabis was readily available, were certainly as young as 14. Is it possible that their parents did not know that the drug was in use, or that it would be consumed at the party?

The case attracted some media attention, though less than it deserved. This was probably because it was not as surprising to media executives and reporters as it was to older citizens who believed that the drug laws were still being enforced. Newspapers were for the most part not shocked at all that cannabis was being smoked by 14- and 15-year-olds in a middle-class home in a fashionable and comfortable district of London. What shock there was, which was mild, was aimed at the stock of other drugs in Mr Dodgeon's house, including ketamine and the MDMA ('Ecstasy') which appears to have killed Miss Jones-Reilly. According to the prosecuting lawyer, Howard Tobias, Mr Dodgeon's 14-year-old daughter found the MDMA when she searched her father's room for marijuana and discovered a container with his drugs 'at the back of a high-up cupboard'.

Mr Dodgeon, plainly and understandably overcome with remorse and regret, later attempted to kill himself by throwing himself off a bridge over a motorway, sustaining severe injuries as a result. The outsider can only feel terrible pity for him, as well as dismay at his willingness to keep dangerous, illegal drugs in a family home. He lived in a milieu in which it was normal and acceptable to take such drugs, and in which the law was widely ignored and the police not expected to enforce it. Had the tragedy not happened (and the chances of it happening were small) his illegal stash would never have been found. Mr Dodgeon, a white-haired, respectable-looking professional of the sixties generation, described himself to police as 'an old hippy'.

Could any of these conditions have existed if the laws against drugs in this country were sternly enforced, as the decriminalisation campaigners incessantly claim that they are?

The first thought to occur is that our society is more corrupted and demoralised by drugs than anyone could possibly have imagined would be the case in 1970. The second is that this demoralisation, concentrated in well-off, articulate and influential layers of our society, has an effect on political and media attitudes. I do not think it unreasonable to suggest that there are many parents like Mr Dodgeon in London and in other parts of the country, who have not been found out.

They are permissive to themselves and their young, personally corrupted by the drug culture. They are furiously and self-interestedly opposed to any tightening of the drug laws. They are a constituency.

The power of this constituency may not yet have reached its high tide. There have been some signs in the last few years that the opponents of drug legalisation are better-organised and more forceful than they have been for some time, and media support for cannabis decriminalisation may actually have diminished slightly since the publication of the Runciman report.

But the growing acceptance of the formulae of the drugs lobby is extraordinarily widespread and reaches very high. As an example of the difficulties faced by any government which wished to take a different course, it is worth studying the period in 2002 which ended with the publication of the House of Commons Select Committee's report on drugs. The involvement of the Prince of Wales with the Runciman committee has already been mentioned. Even the Heir to the Throne and his sons, cannot have been completely insulated from the penetration of British culture by drugs, and by the attitudes which accompany their use.

In May 2002 the nation learned the views on cannabis of Lord Bingham, the former Lord Chief Justice. He told the *Spectator* magazine that he supported a Commons committee in demanding a dramatic relaxation of Britain's drug laws.

Asked if cannabis should be legalised, he said, 'Absolutely. It is stupid having a law which isn't doing what it is there for'. Lord Bingham endorsed the Runciman Report. When asked by an astonished *Daily Telegraph* whether the report was correct, he 'said he thought it probably was. "I think I probably did say that I thought one should concentrate on hard drugs"'. It is particularly interesting that a senior judge, who is in a good position to know how gently the law against cannabis is now enforced, should be unaware that cannabis use was already barely regarded as a crime by the police or the courts. It is even more striking that he should reach for this cliché that abandoning the law against cannabis would release resources for dealing with supposedly 'hard drugs'. The unfailing effectiveness of the promotion of cannabis as 'soft' is beautifully illustrated by this episode.

On the same day the Church of England's Board for 'Social Responsibility' had argued more or less the same thing. The Church was careful to stress that it did not desire actual legalisation, but reclassification of cannabis as a class 'C' drug with possession a non-arrestable offence. This is of course the same thing in reality, but the liberalisers' cunning abstention from open calls for legal drugs enables them to pose as thoughtful moderates. Very few people, probably including the well-intentioned clerics of the 'Board for Social Responsibility', understand how unimportant the distinction really is.

The occasion for this new frenzy of pro-drug sentiment among the elite was the report of the House of Commons Home Affairs Select Committee, chaired by the independent-minded but strongly left-inclined Labour MP (and future Minister) Christopher Mullin. The

Committee had argued for the 'downgrading' of several drugs, and also for 'shooting galleries' in which heroin could be used without fear of arrest, in hygienic circumstances. In general, its conclusions were helpful to those who argued that large-scale drug taking was inevitable, and the most civilised response would therefore be to reduce the harm it did.

It argued 'if there is any single lesson from the experience of the last 30 years, it is that policies based wholly or mainly on enforcement are destined to fail'. It said that attempts by customs and police to restrict supply had largely failed, adding, rather contradictorily, 'The best that can be said is that we have succeeded in containing the problem'. Containment would presumably have made the problem smaller than it would otherwise have been, and have shown that such actions could be effective even if they fell short of complete success.

The committee continued its defeatist direction by arguing – as the advocates of 'harm reduction' had hoped they would – that even if they are advised against it, large numbers of young people will still take drugs. 'In most cases', they intoned complacently 'this is a passing phase which they will grow out of and, while such use should never be condoned, it rarely results in any long-term harm … It therefore makes sense to give priority to educating such young people in harm minimisation rather than prosecuting them'.

Once again, the possible alternative, of a strong deterrent law, is simply not considered. The law is said to have failed, it is presumed to have done so despite having been forcefully applied, it is therefore laid aside. The idea that effective prosecution might be a deterrent is apparently not considered, though in recent times governments have applied this principle to reduce drunken driving and enforce the wearing of seat belts; they have also used powerful civil law deterrents to make smoking unlawful in almost all public buildings, including bars and public houses, despite the sharp unpopularity of this move with both pub landlords and customers.

The committee – of course – did not support legalisation of any drugs. The appearance of responsible moderation and 'realism' must always be maintained by the authors of such reports. But they offered a large sympathetic wink to those who did argue for legalisation. They said it was a course supported by 'many sensible and thoughtful people' adding that 'it may well be that in years to come a future generation will take a different view.

The media reports of the Committee were largely similar. They did not mention the lone but determined attempts by one Conservative MP, Mrs Angela Watkinson, to alter its direction.

Most crucially, she sought to insert the following paragraph:

> We have heard how a softening of enforcement leads very quickly to increased dealing and use: the Lambeth experiment and The Netherlands. The evidence from Sweden, however, has demonstrated how a robust combination of prevention, education and enforcement has resulted in a dramatic reduction in demand that in turn has affected supply. Sweden has sought to create a drug-free society through prevention and police control, following the failure of its previous liberal harm reduction policy. Public opinion in Sweden is very supportive of this policy. The evidence base for the effectiveness of enforcement measures is strong. For example, Swedish policy has demonstrated that stronger enforcement reduces demand and therefore dealing.

The minutes simply say this was 'put and negatived' and record no vote. But an indication of the overwhelmingly defeatist composition of the committee is given soon afterwards in another contest where Mrs Watkinson stood out against her fellow MPs. Legalisation, as all pro-drug campaigners know, is impossible in a national context because of international treaties. So they steer away from calls for national legalisation. But they are quite prepared to seek *international* moves towards open legalisation and 'regulation', the fashionable new term for legalisation, used by pro-drug campaigners because the word suggests a responsible regime.

So when they came to discuss Paragraph 267, the issue was clear. The paragraph read 'We recommend that the Government initiates a discussion within the[1] Commission on Narcotic Drugs of alternative ways – including the possibility of legalisation and regulation – to tackle the global drugs dilemma'.

Mrs Watkinson proposed an amendment to leave out the reference to 'legalisation and regulation'. It was a straight test of strength between those who ultimately favoured legalisation, and those who did not.

She was alone. All the other members present – including David Cameron – voted to retain the significant words. Mrs Watkinson, however, was determined to register her dissent. She proposed to insert a passage of disagreement:

> There is little doubt that illegal drug use is widespread and is the cause of a great deal of acquisitive and violent crime as well as health problems and social misery.
>
> Illegal drug use affects not just users but also their families, friends and the wider community. It is a personal freedom that cannot be exercised without impinging on the freedom of others and, therefore, cannot be tolerated.

There are two alternatives, Mrs Watkinson continued, 'greater acceptance and tolerance or stronger enforcement'. The 'more liberal

---

[1] International.

approach' is justified, she pointed out, by saying that enforcement is impossible:

> This is the policy of surrender and defeat. The same argument could be used to justify decriminalising burglary or speeding. There is no overwhelming public demand in favour of a major relaxation of current anti-drug laws. The answer is not to give in but to step up enforcement and prevention. Prevalence will not decline while users know that there are no sanctions. The example of The Netherlands demonstrates this.
>
> Our first duty is to protect young people from becoming the next generation of drug addicts. Much more robust education and prevention programmes are needed to enable children to reject peer pressure to experiment with drugs. This should include personal responsibility for decision making. Most new users are introduced to the habit by 'friends' and they need to be taught how to resist emotional blackmail.
>
> Robust enforcement regimes in New York and Sweden have been shown to succeed. They could also succeed here. Penalties should be severe enough to deter and should include mandatory drug treatment ... Drug use should not be made easier by simply maintaining habits. Treatment should have withdrawal or abstinence as its goal, otherwise the flow of addicts would never decrease ...
>
> Drugs are illegal for a very good reason—they are harmful. Government should not shrink from upholding existing drug laws and from enforcing them rigorously. However distant the goal might be, government should be aiming for a drug-free society.

I quote this at length because it is, in a way, Mrs Watkinson's minority report and contains many of the arguments which the British establishment have ignored or overridden for the past 40 years. I also quote it because it was once again 'negatived' without the need for a recorded vote. Mrs Watkinson had earlier been squashed in the same way when she attempted to rebut the ancient 'What about alcohol and tobacco?' red herring so much beloved of those who wish to weaken the cannabis laws. Her proposed words 'However, we do not accept the argument that because alcohol and tobacco are legal and have acknowledged risks, drugs should also be made legal' were not allowed into the report. Nor could she win support for this sentence, a straightforward statement of fact 'Cannabis is also known to be a risk factor for schizophrenia and to affect levels of attainment in students, performance at work, the ability to drive safely, judgement and insight'.

The full clash is available in the published minutes of the Committee and is an interesting summary of many of the arguments between conservatives and 'libertarians' on this subject. More interesting by far is that fact that in all but a very few votes, the conservative position – though intellectually respectable and widespread among voters – is represented by only one member of one party in an all-party committee of 11 men and women.

The committee's final meeting on the drugs issue[2] was in effect a running battle between Mrs Watkinson and her colleagues. At the end of it she refused to vote for the report as a whole, a highly unusual step for a Committee member to take. By any standards, this was an interesting event in politics, presumably worth some mention. Yet at the time it was barely noticed or recorded in media reports. Why should it have been? There was no real desire for a proper debate on principle. The only views deemed worth of reporting were those in favour of the agreed elite policy, of hollowing out the law while pretending to uphold it. And from time to time that elite may also

---

[2] On Thursday 9 May 2002.

complain that the law is oppressive, and its oppressive nature is the cause of the problems we face, and Sir Simon Jenkins can be summoned to his keyboard to write another libertarian tirade, which will make the government look responsible and cautious.

And so the law is diluted a little more, and we return to Barbara Wootton's bold but justified prediction that 'the laughable idealism of one generation' will 'evolve into the accepted commonplace of the next'.

That prophecy was made in an England as unimaginable to most of us, as the place we now live in, the country formerly known as Great Britain, would have been unimaginable to our fellow countrymen, going about their business on the morning of 26 February 1970 when – all unknown to them – a Cabinet meeting voted to call off the war on drugs, but to pretend it was still fighting it. The pretence continues.

Index

Abrams, Stephen (Steve)
  on battle of West Wittering 106
  claims cannabis use rife at Oxford 100
  clear-eyed account of later developments in decriminalisation 160
  comments on Sergeant Pepper album 117
  described 1967 as 'watershed year' for cannabis 99
  engaging memoir 129
  explains background to *Times* advertisement 129–32
  his assessment contrasted with that of Sir Simon Jenkins 210
  purses lips 115
  role in advertisement in *The Times* 96
  runs SOMA 129
  still influences conventional wisdom today 130
  suggests subtle campaign 114
  urges advertisement in *The Times* 115
  writes obituary of Bing Spear 63
abuse, usual, author prepares for xii
ACMD (Advisory Council – sometime Committee – on the Misuse of Drugs)
  David Nutt, member of 200
  Hans-Christian Raabe removed from, on spurious grounds 201
  keeps law on drugs under constant review 201
ACPO (Association of Chief Police Officers in England and Wales)
  accurately described as policymaking body 215
  circulated forces with news of 'success' of Paddick scheme 224
  recommends 'Cannabis Warning' as preferred response to illegal possession 200
  unable to give clear answer on origin of 'Cannabis Warning' 201
Adderall, drug given to healthy children by badly-behaved adults x
addiction
  authorities severely inconsistent about 247
  cannot be objectively diagnosed 18
  portrayed in film *French Connection 2* 18
  cited as excuse for crime by police 246
  concept which abolishes free will, examined 18–19

concept's curious logic examined
    245–6
  essentially circular 18
  widely accepted by courts 245
Afghan farmer, treated very
    differently from his Opium-
    growing counterpart in
    Oxfordshire 9
Ainsworth, Peter, confesses cannabis
    use 170
Ainsworth, Robert (former Labour
    Cabinet minister) not
    reluctant to be linked with
    liberalisation 89
Ali, Tariq, signs advertisement in *The
    Times* 97
antidepressants, astonishing numbers
    of prescriptions for 10
alcohol
  Anthony Crosland seeks
      liberalisation of licensing laws
      56
  greater use possibly side-effect of
      prevalence of powerful illegal
      drugs 241
  loosening of licensing laws
      desired by cultural
      revolutionaries 10
  successfully restricted by 1915
      licensing law 56
  scrapping of 1915 laws followed
      by much increased use 56
Alcoholics Anonymous, credited for
    discovery that people who do
    not want to give something up
    will generally fail to do so 19
American Psychiatric Association
  once classified homosexuality as a
      disorder, now doesn't 22
  produces manual for diagnosing
      mental complaints 22

Angell, Dr Marcia, challenges
    orthodox certainties on
    treatment of 'depression' 20
Attenborough, David (BBC2
    Controller)
  said to have complained of
      'distinct smell of weed' in BBC
      studios 120
  said to have told staff to get it
      'under control' 120
Attention Deficit Hyperactivity
    Disorder (ADHD) made-up
    disease lacking objective
    symptoms, invented to
    explain bad schools and poor
    parenting x
Ayer, Freddie, expresses doubts
    about happy drugs and harm
    principle 95

Bakewell, Baroness Joan
  in adulterous relationship 120
  praises David Attenborough 120
  recalls that others smoked
      cannabis in BBC studios 120
Barker, Paul
  points out Runciman didn't call
      for decriminalisation 206
  writes approvingly about Paddick
      experiment 205
BBC
  calls painter into studio after
      unexpected swing to Tories in
      1970 election 75
  open law-breaking by cannabis
      users permitted on premises
      120
Beatles, The (a popular musical
    combination)
  awarded MBEs 122
  release *Sergeant Pepper,* 117

trod careful line between raucousness and respectability 118
Beaverbrook, Lord (Max Aitken), owner of *Daily Express* 37
Benn, Anthony Wedgwood (later Tony), votes for liberalisation of drugs in decisive Cabinet meeting (1970) 73
Benson (RAF station in Southern England) not required to napalm opium fields nearby 9
Betts, Janet (Mrs) given special licence by media to speak against drug culture because of bereavement 204
Betts, Leah, died horribly after taking ecstasy 204
Bingham, Lord (former Lord Chief Justice)
   asked by astonished *Daily Telegraph* if report correct 262
   emits conventional wisdom 262
   gives views on drugs to *Spectator* magazine 262
Birmingham, Anthony Crosland wants to make it more like Paris 90
Blackwood, Nicola (Conservative MP) obtains rare figures of arrests and disposals for class 'A' drug abusers 234
Blair, Anthony, said to have reassured Janet Betts that drugs would not be legalized 204
Blair, Ian (Metropolitan Police Commissioner)
   blusters about middle class drug abusers 239
   embarrassed by Rausing case 239

Bloom, Allan
   connects drugs and rock music 7–9
   cry of despair at slow death of education 7
   warns that drugs break link between effort and delight 110
Bloomsbury, influence hugely increased by power of TV 119
Blunkett, David (Labour Politician) as Home Secretary provides cover for Paddick project 212
Bottoms, A. E. (criminologist) queries figures on numbers of cannabis users sent to prison 127–8
Brave New World
   Huxley fears we are embracing one xi
   may be rather nasty when it arrives 110
Bradford, Anthony Crosland wants to make it more like Paris 90
Brady, Ian 109
Broken Windows Principle
   Belief that enforcing minor laws necessary to ensure compliance with law in general, contradicted by claims that abandoning pursuit of 'minor' drug offences 'frees up' police 164
Brook, Peter, signs advertisement in *The Times* 97
burglary
   police would have much less to do if it were legalized 14
   victims of it distressed and angry 15
bus drivers, among other honest people forced by government to buy stupefying drugs for criminal parasites 17

Index

Butt, Ronald
    fooled by militant anti-drug rhetoric of governments 210
    mocked in *The Times* by Barbara Wootton for misunderstanding drug law developments 162

Cabinet
    calls off war on drugs, while pretending to carry on fighting it 268
    deliberation of on drugs incoherent 10
    split between working class conservative Labour ministers, and university-educated radical Labour ministers 65
    surrenders to drug liberalizing lobby before lunch 13
Cairncross, Frances (notable advocate of drug decriminalization), typical figure of new liberal establishment 39
Callaghan, James (former Home Secretary)
    acts to forestall Wootton Report 134
    described in *Sunday Mirror* as having had 'dramatic change of mind on drugs' 71
    enters lowly branch of civil service 71
    grasps that cannabis lobby will not call openly for legalisation 136
    has little in common with Crossman 71
    has scorn dripped upon him by Richard Crossman 70–1
    leaks story on Cabinet split to *Sunday Mirror* 61
    makes direct attack on Roy Jenkins and 'Permissive Society' 135–6
    meets wife while Sunday School teacher 71
    never finishes task 81
    never to be Home Secretary again 82
    not clear if Callaghan was truly overruled by colleagues 71
    opposes distinction between cannabis and other dangerous drugs 77
    possible cunning of leak by 71
    prosaic and far from liberal 71
    puts up last stand against liberalisers in Cabinet 77
    remains faithful to wife all his life 71
    serves in Royal Navy 71
    shows promise at school 71
    stands for everything Crossman disliked about his own party 71
    suggests higher penalty for cannabis possession 77
    thought it pointless to argue against Misuse of Drugs Act on principle 73
    told to introduce Misuse of Drugs Bill to Parliament 81
    university hopes dashed by father's early death 71
Cameron, David (MP, member of House of Commons Home Affairs Committee) later Coalition Prime Minister
    aides with drug liberalisers on Home Affairs Committee 265

even he has not yet enacted or supported Sir Simon Jenkins's ideas 21
cannabis (marijuana)
  associated with various episodes of criminal violence 47–51
  British establishment wishes to minimize dangers of 25
  a cause as well as a drug 3
  decriminalised in all but name 224
  defenders dismiss quantities of worrying information as anecdotal 27
  fate of ordinary (non-celebrity) users in 1967 101–2
  figures on arrest and convictions (1967–2009) 99–100
  figures on arrests for possession 151
  given special legal status by 'A, B, C' classification 29
  ill-effects felt by people other than the user 27
  indefensible complacency of legalisation lobby 25
  its drowsy fumes frowned on by Christian-based law 88
  its relation to other drugs not comparable to relation of 'soft' drinks to alcohol 80
  its use correlated with mental illness 19
  Labour's plans to decriminalize in all but name 64
  maximum penalty for possession yet again reduced (1976) 160
  medical absurdity of 'self-medication' with 23
  mentally-ill users not detected by conventional statistics 23
  misleadingly described as 'soft' 80
  not necessarily a peace-promoting drug 47–51
  officially less dangerous than heroin or LSD 81
  permanent and irrecoverable setbacks to users' school careers 27
  principal active ingredient identified 27
  reclassified as Class 'C' drug 212
  Thatcher government weakens laws against 163–4
  those plans adopted wholesale by Tory Party 64
  users insist it has done them no harm 27
  wildly varying estimates of levels of use 145
cannabis warning (non-punitive, unrecorded police disposal of breach of cannabis possession law, used to deal with bulk of cannabis cases by 2007) 79
  86, 953 issued in 2009 200
  not recorded centrally 200
  preferred response of ACPO to cannabis possession 200
  quietly introduced 224
Carr, Robert (Home Secretary) makes complacent statement on drug problem (1973) 146
Castle, Barbara, voted for liberalisation in crucial 1970 Cabinet meeting 73
Charles, Prince of Wales, reported to have supported Runciman inquiry 176
  cannot have been wholly insulated from drug culture 261

Chiltern Hills, opium poppies
    flourish on 9
Christianity
    allied with Labour 88
    basis of puritan objections to
        drug-taking 88
    insists on eternal reward 88
    scorns self-indulgence 88
    Soma has all the advantages of,
        none of the drawbacks of 83
Christian morals, almost gone 4
    giving way at edges 125
Church of England, its 'Board
    for Social Responsibility'
    embraces the fashion for drug
    decriminalisation 262
cigarettes
    comparison of laws on tobacco
        with laws on cannabis 58
    first linked to lung cancer in
        Hitler-era Germany 31
    importance of law's restrictions
        on possession and use, not
        just on supply 58
    not sold by chemists 16
    popular disgust at smell of
        burning tobacco aids laws
        restricting their use 57
    success of those laws thanks to
        enforcement 57
Clarke, Charles (Home Office
    Minister) said to have
    rejected slightest whiff of
    reform 206
class 'A' drugs, figures on penalties
    imposed for abusers 234–5
classification of dangerous drugs,
    owes far more to politics than
    to science 29
    rightly mocked by Professor
        David Nutt 80

anti-drug campaigners lured into
    futile campaigns for tougher
    classification 80
Clergymen, support drug legalisation
    7
Closing of the American Mind, Allan
    Bloom's cry of despair, 7
cocaine, bad effects of on human
    beings 16
    cannabis has greater risk of doing
        irreversible damage than 29
Cockburn, Henry, placed in locked
    ward, taking antipsychotic
    medication, life radically
    altered for the worse, possible
    that use of cannabis to blame
    19, 195
Cockburn, Patrick: *Henry's Demons,* 19
    describes son Henry's mental
        illness following cannabis use
        19
Conservative and Unionist Party
    adopts 'progressive' policies of
        Labour's cultural and moral
        left 64
    elite forms alliance with Labour
        elite against conservative-
        minded members and
        supporters of both parties 82
    readier than Labour to pursue
        drug liberalization 252
Cornwell, John, quotes A. J. Ayer on
    Huxley 94
crackdown, word invariably presaging
    inaction and retreat 205
Creamcheese, Suzy, not admired by
    elderly 125
Crick, Francis, signs advertisement
    in *The Times* 97
crime, people's dislike of being
    victims of it 15

Crosland, Anthony, creator of new
society 9
  cry from the heart for brighter
  Britain 89
  Future of Socialism 64
  his ideas lead to loosening of
  alcohol laws 56
  his views on personal liberation
  may have helped Labour win
  1964 election 94
  laughs at Beatrice and Sidney
  Webb 93
  seeks civilised society 56
  voted for liberalisation in decisive
  Cabinet meeting 73
  wants Britain to be more
  colourful 89
Crossman, Richard H. S., progenitor
of new society 9
  adventurous sexual life 69
  attempted recruitment into
  Comintern 70
  describes self as 'modern
  unconventional' 70
  drips scorn on Callaghan 70-1
  hides existence of first wife in
  Who's Who 70
  hypocritical complaint against
  Callaghan's leaks 7
  libel action against the *Spectator*
  70
  Louche troublemaker records
  class split in Labour Cabinet
  in diaries 61
  slightly distorts truth 65
  social liberal and libertine 69
  son of Tory judge 69
  voted for liberalisation in decisive
  Cabinet meeting (1970) 73
  was black propagandist during
  Second World War 71
  was intellectual snob 71
Cultural Revolution, quiescent in
1970s 78
  Central Committee of 97
  picks up speed 99

Daily Express, once-influential
national newspaper 37
Daily Mail, calls for 'debate' on
Runciman report 189
Daily Telegraph, no longer organ of
reaction 191
  sympathetic to Runciman report
  and to drug liberalisation
  191
Dalyrymple, Theodore, casts doubts
on myth of insuperable
physical addiction 18
decriminalisation – of drugs will lead
to doped contentment and
willing serfdom xi
  advocates of it pretend for
  propaganda purposes 11
  campaigners for it knew what
  they were doing 10
  never confused socialism with
  social liberalism 43
  will create apathy 11
  will undermine competent,
  efficient society 11
  depression epidemic of this
  accompanies development of
  drugs claiming to treat it 21
Deedes, William (Later Lord
Deedes), makes liberal
defeatist speech 137
Dennis, Norman, attacks use of Mill
by drug liberalisers 43
Diamond, Jack, voted for drug
liberalisation in decisive
Cabinet meeting (1970) 73

Dimbleby, David, signs advertisement in *The Times* 97
Dodgeon, Brian, tragic case of 259
Doherty, Peter, had 21 previous drug offences to name 235
    drops heroin on floor of court building 236
    has large number of suits 237
    is not sent to prison 237
    may not choose own clothes 237
Doll, Sir Richard, scientist, who gave up smoking long before link between smoking and lung cancer was officially accepted, 31
    reports sharp rise on deaths, correlated with increase in smoking 33
Donovan (Donovan Philips Leitch) appears on TV 102
    arrest in comical circumstances with attractive blonde 101
    fined £250 103
    not enjoying respectable evening at home 103
    tried, not imprisoned 102, 106
    sings 'Sunshine Superman' 105
Driberg, Tom, MP, signs advertisement in *The Times* 97
drug dealers, mysteriously classified as evil while consumers and buyers are not, example in Tory Manifesto (2001) 173
drunken driving, enforcement of laws against this consistently and sternly enforced 58
    contrasted with comparable weakness of law and government publicity directed against illegal drugs 58

DSM (Diagnostic and Statistical Manual) accepted standard for mental health diagnoses 22
    shifting diagnoses in 22
Dunkirk, compared to police retreat in the face of illegal drugs, disguised as a triumph 213
Dyslexia, contentious complaint lacking objective physical or biochemical diagnosis 21

economic crisis, likely to be permanent 5
Economist, The, supporter of policies based on J. S. Mill and the 'harm principle' 39
    carries leak of Runciman report, 176
    supports decriminalisation of drugs 40
ecstasy, premature (experienced by drug users) 7
ecstasy, (MDMA) illegal drug blamed for death of Leah Betts 204
    blamed for death of Isobel Jones-Reilly 259
Egypt, disastrous results of widespread cannabis use in 5
Emory Wheel, American University newspaper, interviews Keith Stroup 226
Epstein, Brian, Beatles manager's involvement in *Times* advertisement 116
European Common Market (earlier name for European Union), media preoccupied with during 1970s 78
Evening Standard, London newspaper, reports on Paddick experiment 203

examinations, passed without reading texts under discussion 4

Fienburgh, Wilfred, MP, his novel wrongly neglected 54
free will, abolished by acceptance of concept of 'addiction' 18
freedom to take drugs opposite of freedom of thought xi
freeing up, claim that Police will be 'freed up' for other tasks invariably made as pretext for ceasing to pursue possession, direct contradiction of 'Broken Windows' principle 164
   claim hard to check 213
   examined 213
French Connection 2, film absurdly portraying heroin addiction as near-insuperable 18
French students in revolt xi
Friend, Judge Gordon, sentences 'Hoppy' Hopkins to prison, saying he is 'a pest to society' 113
Fuller, Mike (Deputy Assistant Commissioner, Metropolitan Police) says 'no question' Paddick experiment will be abandoned 219
   records worries about message to schoolchildren 221
Future of Socialism: Anthony Crosland writes to set out socially revolutionary programme 1956, calls for general change in cultural attitudes 89

Gardiner, Gerald, votes for liberalisation at decisive Cabinet meeting 73

Garnett, Tony, signs advertisement in *The Times* 97
General Election of 1970 74–5
   ejects James Callaghan from Home Office 81
General Practice Research Database, may omit significant numbers of mentally-disturbed cannabis users 24
Germany, scientists in Hitler era linked cigarettes and lung cancer 31
gibberish, contradictory – characterisation of post-1970 UK drugs policy 10
gin, not sold by chemists 16
Godber, Sir George, complains of 'incessant propaganda' for cigarettes 36
Golden Calf, majority preference for worship of 94
Gorbachev, Mikhail Sergeyevich (former General Secretary of Soviet Communist Party and President of Soviet Union) his failed alcohol ban results mainly in sugar shortage 57
Goring Gap, fields of opium poppies run down to Thames at 9
Gove, Michael (Education Secretary) was near neighbour of Brian Dodgeon 259
gratification deferred, Protestant insistence on abandoned 88
Greene, Graham, signs advertisement in *The Times* 97
Greene, Hugh Carleton (Director General of BBC, Brother of Graham) cultural revolutionary 121

Hague, William, leader of
   Conservative Party
   details of his 1973 speech ending
      imprisonment for cannabis
      possession 145–6
Hailsham of Marylebone, Lord
   (Quintin Hogg), defends
   tobacco curbs 33
   will tell magistrates to soften
      cannabis sentencing 74
   punished for dabbling with
      conservative policies 168
   supports Callaghan's caution on
      liberalisation 135
   this instruction would have been
      made impossible if Cabinet had
      voted for higher penalties 78
Hardcastle, Sally, interviews Barbara
   Wootton 134
Harris, Rufus, Honours Graduate of
   'Bing Spear University' 63
Harrogate, planned site of laboratory
   for research into tobacco
   safety 33
Havers, Michael powerful legal
   representation for Jagger and
   Richards 107
Healey, Denis, votes for
   liberalisation at decisive
   Cabinet meeting 73
Heath, Sir Edward
   attacked for Misuse of Drugs Act
      by Sir Simon Jenkins 211
   his Cabinet absorbs and accepts
      Labour's drug liberalisation
      plans without amendment 64
Heaven, Kingdom of, Britain ceases
   to believe in 88
Hegel, Georg Wilhelm, his writings
   enjoyed by Reginald Maudling
   82

Hellawell, Keith, 'drugs czar', said
   to issue assurances that
   drugs will never be legalized
   204
Her Majesty's Government, licenses
   opium poppy crops in
   Oxfordshire 9
heroin
   cannabis more likely to do
      irreversible damage than 29
   figures on abuse of 100
   undesirable effects of on human
      beings 16–17
Hindley, Myra 109
Hockney, David, signs advertisement
   in *The Times* 97
Hoey, Kate, Labour MP
   personally offered 'skunk' in
      street 222
   says Paddick scheme has
      undermined law and order,
      says drugs now sold openly in
      Brixton 222
Holy Trinity, not nowadays accepted
   as arbiter on morals 39
homeless, people known
   misleadingly as 23
Hopkins, John 'Hoppy', his
   imprisonment alarms
   liberated London 112–13
House of Commons Home Affairs
   Committee
   Angela Watkinson lone voice on
      264
   chaired by Christopher Mullin
      262
   conclusions helpful to defeatists
      263
   currently making new inquiry
      250
   easily led by liberalisers 213

Howarth, Gerald, MP, warns that Paddick warning policy will send wrong signal 205
Hughes, Cledwyn, votes against liberalisation at decisive Cabinet meeting 73
Huxley, Aldous, warns of willing self-stupefaction by modern societies xi
   meant *Brave New World* to be a warning 85
   predicts threat to liberty from hedonism 85–6
   quoted on hedonistic freedom versus political liberty 1
   quoted on Soma 83

Indian Hemp Commission, prehistoric 1894 inquiry into cannabis, cited by Wootton Report 28, 149
Indica Bookshop, counterculture outpost, name explained 113
   emergency meeting at 113
informers, drug user's fear of largely removed by 1971 Act 66
Inglis, Brian, signs advertisement in *The Times* 97
International Times (IT), culturally radical magazine 112
   threatened with closure 113
Iran, Islamic Republic of. Fails to stamp out long-established Persian culture of wine-drinking 57
Ironsides, Cromwellian soldiers, liberty arose from their puritanism 112
Iversen, Professor Leslie, not among conservatives in debate on drug laws 230
   warns of difficulties of establishing medical benefits of cannabis 230

Jagger, Sir Michael
   bailed 117
   gives interview to *Daily Mirror* 108
   Metropolitan Police drugs squad declines to arrest 10
   provoked into libel suit by *News of the World* 101
   Wittering raid leads to trial, imprisonment and ultimate acquittal of 107
Jaggerism, assertion of total sovereignty over our own bodies invention of 111
Jenkin, Bernard, confesses cannabis use 169
Jenkins, Lord (Roy), progenitor of new society 9
   appointed Dame Ruth Runciman to key post 175
   appoints Barbara Wootton 115
   did not expect her to produce conservative report 142
   prefers term 'civilised society' to 'permissive society' 64
   sets out revolutionary programme in *The Labour Case* 64
Jenkins, Sir Simon (former editor of *The Times* and proponent of drug liberalization) 89
   blames Misuse of Drugs Act for drug-ridden nature of London 210
   equates Misuse of Drugs Act with American Prohibition of alcohol 211

has he been fooled by militant anti-drug rhetoric of governments? 210
his beliefs reflected in Runciman report 184
on Runciman committee 180
says Act has 'failed completely' 210
urges legal conduits for drug trade 211
Jesus Christ (Saviour of Mankind, Son of God)
drank wine at last supper 56
turned water into wine at Cana in Galilee 56
Johnson, Pamela Hansford, attends Brady and Hindley trial, writes *On Iniquity*, influences C. P. Snow 109
Jones, Brian, arrested for cannabis possession 107

Keele University Study on cannabis and mental health may have missed important numbers of mentally disturbed cannabis users 24
King George VI, those who asserted role of smoking in his death ridiculed 35

Labour Party more cautious than Tories about open moves to liberalise drugs 252
National Executive of 1956 described by Crosland as morally sterner than the bench of bishops 90
party elite forms effective alliance with Tories against own members 82
transformed into metropolitan radical grouping 65
La Guardia, Fiorello, sometime Mayor of New York City. His obsolete 1944 report on 'marihuana' cited in Wootton Report 28, 149
Laing, R. D., signs advertisement in *The Times* 97
Lansley, Andrew (Conservative politician), does not call for resignation of Marjorie Mowlam after she reveals drug use while superintending anti-drug policy 177
law, cause of crime (according to drug liberalisers) 11
Leather, Ted, MP, dismisses anti-tobacco campaign as 'hysterical nonsense' 32
has cigarette factory in constituency 32
Letwin, Oliver, says used cannabis accidentally at university 171
Lawson, Lord Nigel, says NHS is closest thing Britain has to religion 59
Left, cannot have foreseen things they would bring about xi
blame others for failure, rather than change principles xi
Lever, Harold, votes for liberalisation at decisive Cabinet meeting 73
Licensing Laws, 1915 British restriction on alcohol sales, more effective than US alcohol Prohibition 56
relaxed in 1980s 56
Lilley, Peter, MP (Former Conservative Minister)
fails to distinguish between law being unenforced, and law being unenforceable 253

feels no reluctance in siding with
    liberalization 89
knows better 256
may have sought popularity among
    readers of *The Guardian* 253
mistakes formal penalties for real
    behaviour of police and courts
    256
positioning of facts in pamphlet
    highly significant 258
publishes foolish pamphlet 253
says decriminalisation of cannabis
    'inevitable' 253
turns logic upside down 255
LSD, dangers of cannabis comparable
    to dangers to 29

Malik, Michael Abdul ('Michael X')
    signs advertisement in *The
    Times* 97
  hanged for murder 97
marijuana *see* cannabis; medical
    marijuana
Maschler, Tom, signs advertisement
    in *The Times* 97
Mason, C. W. defends tobacco
    smoking 32
Mason, Roy, votes against liberalisation
    at crucial Cabinet meeting 73
Maude, Francis, confesses cannabis
    use 169
Maudling, Reginald MP, takes over
    Misuse of Drugs Act unaltered
    from outgoing Labour
    government 82
  had more in common with
    Crossman than with
    Callaghan 82
  shows clear understanding of
    Misuse of Drugs Act's purpose
    136

MacIntyre, Alasdair, signs
    advertisement in *The Times*
    97
Macleod, Ian, issues first ministerial
    warning on health risks of
    smoking 34
McCartney, Sir Paul, said to be
    'horrified' by imprisonment of
    'Hoppy' Hopkins 115
  organizes payment for *Times*
    advertisement 116
  lobbying skills 116
McKeganey, Professor Neil,
    *Controversies in Drugs, policy
    and practice,* 247
  criticisms of harm reduction and
    rehabilitation policies 248–9
  says drugs issue fundamentally a
    moral one 250
medical marijuana
  arguments against 225–6
  campaigners for never distance
    themselves from campaign for
    looser laws 231
  described as 'Red Herring to
    give marijuana a good name',
    in 1979, by liberalisation
    campaigner Keith Stroup 227
  makes cannabis more easily
    available to healthy people
    230
  strange self-defeating support
    of campaigners for general
    relaxation laws 226
  strengthened campaign for
    decriminalisation 230–1
  success in persuading American
    states 229
mental illness, vagueness and
    subjectivity of diagnoses 20
methadone

£300 million annual cost of
supplying it to takers of illegal
drugs 17
ineffective in use 248
sold by recipients to pay for
heroin 18
Micawber, Wilkins, many Oxford
students have never heard of 5
Michael, George, freed with caution
after arrest in possession of
drugs 240
Miles, Barry, author of *Many Years
from Now* 107
on John 'Hoppy' Hopkins 112
praises Paul McCartney's
lobbying skills 116
Mill, John Stuart, cited in support
of right to smoke yourself to
death 35
drug liberalisers use of his
arguments based on
questionable reading 40
invents ASBO 41
On Liberty 39
supports use of law to save
individual from self 41
suffers failure of imagination 41
supposed view on individual
sovereignty supported by
economic and social liberals
252
views regarded as
unchallengeable on staffs of
Fleet Street newspapers 191
milk, intensively marketed
door-to-door product. Do
illegal drugs outperform it?
210
Misuse of Drugs Act, 1971, based on
belief that there is no safe dose
for drugs it outlaws 15

approved by Labour Cabinet as
Misuse of Drugs Bill 65
based on Wootton Report 137–8
bipartisan support 137
Callaghan criticizes defeatism of
138–9
cannabis may have dangers
not suspected at time of its
passing 27
downgrades offence of possession
66
endlessly flexible 224
extraordinary handover of
Bill from Labour to Tory
government, second reading
136
fear of informers largely removed
by, for possessors and users of
illegal drugs 66
from pursuing possessors of
illegal drugs 66–7
gives official support to idea that
cannabis is less harmful than
heroin or LSD 65
much-reduced penalties in Act
discourage Police
survives officially unamended 224
treats cannabis as less serious
than other drugs 65
work in progress 201
'Modern unconventionals', 1930s
radicals sympathetic to drug
liberalisation, Crossman
describes himself as such 70
held on to crucial tents of moral
and cultural revolution 81
Monday Club, right-wing grouping,
author hears members
mouthing propaganda of drug
liberalisers, thinking it was
their own idea 207

Monterey, scene of first major
    outdoor rock festival 113
  significance of 113
'morning-after pill', would have
    outraged morals of 60 years
    ago 16
Moss, Kate, no action taken against
    after images published of her
    snorting white powder 240
Mount Sinai (place of issue of Ten
    Commandments) no longer
    generally accepted as source of
    moral law 39
Mowlam, Marjorie ('Mo')
  endorses unscientific distinction
    between 'hard' and 'soft' drugs
    177
  her public liberalism on drugs
    exceptional in Labour Party,
    and why 252
  her resignation not called for by
    Tory opposite number 177
  reveals past drug use while
    in charge of Government
    anti-drug policy 176–7
Muenzenberg, Willi, attempts to
    recruit Richard Crossman to
    Comintern 70
Muggeridge, Michael, his
    exasperated jeers at
    establishment defenders of
    cannabis 7
Mullin, Christopher (Chairman
    of Home Affairs Select
    Committee) 262
  left-wing 262
Murray, Professor Sir Robin, has
    little doubt about correlation
    between cannabis use and
    mental illness 26
  not a lightweight 26
  view not universally shared in his
    profession 26
mystery of evil nature of drugs,
    present during cultivation,
    transport and sale, but absent
    during possession and use 66

Nanterre, squabble over male access
    to women's dormitory at
    university may have sparked
    May 1968 uprising 109
National Health Service
  cannabis-based medicine
    available through 9
  cash shortage causes it to minimize
    mental illness prevalence 25
needle-sharing, pitifully small effects
    of programme 249
neuropsychopharmacology, curious
    mixture of exact and inexact
    sciences 20
News of the World (defunct Sunday
    newspaper)
  connection to events in West
    Wittering 106
  makes drug claims against rock
    stars 100
  series published 106
Norman, Archie, confesses cannabis
    use, has no regrets 170
Nuns, Maltese, pray over author as
    he is born x
Nutt, Professor David (Professor of
    Neuropsychopharmacology),
    rightly mocks drug
    classifications 80
  author's broadcast clash with him
    199–201

O'Connor, John (former head of
    Scotland Yard Flying Squad)

states cannabis has been decriminalised drug for years 114
appears to have been bamboozled by propaganda 166
Oakland, California, evidence from suggest cannabis harmless 154
Oliver, Jonathan, journalist, his work commended 166
his account quoted at length 169–73
Orwell, George, his book *1984* used as instruction manual by North Korean state 85
Oxford University
graduates obtain degrees despite inability to spell 5
cannabis use said to be rife at in 1967 100
Oxfordshire, opium growing officially encouraged in 10
opium, grown legally in Oxfordshire, 9
Oppositional Defiant Disorder (ODD) author has suffered (or benefited) from, since birth x

Paddick, Brian (former Deputy Assistant Commissioner, Metropolitan Police) 202
criticized 218–19
enterprising and original 202
experiment reported as success 215–16
explains his new warning policy 203
explains workings of his experiment 207
Kate Hoey MP attacks scheme 221–2
negative report stifled 223

'no question' of abandoning experiment 219
officially classified as success 224
police under pressure to prove experiment working 224
success analysed 216–17
paracetamol, cannot be sold directly from shelves when mixed with Codeine 15
Paris, radicals cheering on 1968 French student revolt in xi
Parker, Lord Justice (Lord Chief Justice of England) grants Mick Jagger's appeal 108
Peart, Fred, votes against liberalisation at decisive Cabinet meeting 73
Pilcher, Detective Sergeant Norman ('Nobby')
did not know which way drugs battle was going 107
disgraced 107
mocked as 'Semolina Pilchard' 107
Pincher, Harry Chapman, says risks of cigarettes exaggerated 33
Pilgrim Fathers, their Puritanism led to political liberty 112
Piper, John, signs advertisement in *The Times* 97
pizza, intensively marketed and sold door-to-door. Is it outperformed in this field by drugs? 210
pleasure, search for has replaced pursuit of happiness 3
police
complimented by Ruth Runciman for 'discretion' in enforcing the law 184
discouraged from pursuing cases of drug possession by

much-reduced penalties in 1971 Act 67
ecstasy 214
her report helps to create system under which cannabis possession does not result in criminal record 184
Police Foundation, organisation vaguely connected to the police 176
police officers call for weaker laws against
their enthusiasm for weakening the drug laws, explained 165–6
their fear of being blamed for racial conflict explained 180–1
popular music, lyrics of crammed with drug references 4
pornography, campaign to liberate is ludicrously disguised as battle against censorship 4
Portillo, Michael, Tory politician seen as leader of liberalizing tendency 167–8
refuses to answer questions on past use of cannabis 171
possession of cannabis, downgraded as criminal offence by Misuse of Drugs Act 66
prisons, supposedly under tight control of authorities, 249
drug abuse common in 249
prohibition, term often abused by drug liberalisers 54
cited as argument against enforcement in Wootton Report 149
did not make possession illegal 55
equated with Misuse of Drugs Act 1971 by Sir Simon Jenkins 211

importance of false claim that it is being applied and does not work 79
took place in circumstances unique to US, historically and geographically 55
US prohibition of alcohol utterly unlike modern attempts to restrict illegal drugs 55
Protestant civilisation, deferred reward important in 8
Protestant ethic, regarded as tiresome by moderns 9
Protestantism, Anglo-Saxon, force the cultural revolutionaries all knew they were against 10
New Labour wish to be liberated from 252
psychosis, vagueness of term 25

Raabe, Dr Hans-Christian, removed from ACMD on irrelevant grounds 201
racial bigotry, author's generation expresses scorn for xi
Rausing, Hans Kristian and Eva
charged with possessing cocaine and heroin 238
cannot be attempted simultaneously with punishment 244
cautioned 238
found with drugs in US Embassy 238
not untypical of those caught with such drugs 239
rehabilitation, of users of illegal drugs, concept directly contradicting law and justice 244

Release, organisation formed to help people arrested in possession of illegal drugs 63
  gets support from Jonathan Aitken 63
Rees-Mogg, Lord William
  not so sympathetic to Richards 117
  thought Jagger's amphetamine possession not serious 117
  'Who Breaks a Butterfly upon a Wheel' 117
Rhetoric, militant and noisy, important smokescreen for weakening of drug laws 66
Richards, Keith
  imprisoned on drugs offence, then freed on appeal 107
  says he is not an old man 108
  statement explained 111
  bailed 117
Ross, William, votes against liberalisation at decisive Cabinet meeting 73
Royal Air Force, base at Benson not required to eradicate opium poppies in Oxfordshire 9
Ritalin, drug given to healthy children by badly-behaved adults x
Runciman, Dame Ruth
  accepts that statutory penalties are rarely if ever imposed 185–6
  appointed to Advisory Committee on Misuse of Drugs by Roy Jenkins 175
  inquiry set up in 1997 177
  her committee lacks conservative voice 179
  is applauded for defeatist policy 175
  is 'grateful' to Ann Widdecombe 178
  key member of north London liberal elite 176
  Paul Barker points out that report didn't call for decriminalisation 206
  perceptive and important remarks about liberalisers' room for manoeuvre 183
  publicly acknowledges that penalties in law for cannabis possession not imposed before her inquiry began 182
    after it had begun 184
  refers sympathetically to 'medical cannabis' 229
  report's conclusions 195–7
  reveals congruence between inquiry and Paddick experiment in Brixton 178
  suggests laws only worthwhile if they eradicate crimes against which they are aimed 182
  suggests prosecution of offender worse than crime 181
  this view examined and criticized 182–3
  ultimate do-gooder 175

Sergeant Pepper (record released 1 June 1967) 117
  said to be 'saturated' with drug references 117
Schizophrenia, vagueness of term 25
  explanation needed for doubling of incidence on South London 1965–95 26
Schofield, Michael
  member of Wootton Committee 97
  signs advertisement in *The Times* 97
  this connection little-noticed 162

self, exalted by sex, drugs and rock music 3
  -indulgence, drug taking purest form of 3
  -stupefaction, wrongness of, and legal implications of this 65–6
'Sex, Drugs and Rock and Roll' tripod on which modern morality rests 3
Shackleton, Lord, votes for liberalisation at decisive Cabinet meeting 73
Shore, Peter, votes for liberalisation at decisive Cabinet meeting 73
Sinclair of Cleeve, Lord, (President of Imperial Tobacco) says link between cancer and smoking not proven 33
Snow, C. P. (novelist and politician) discusses moral decline in *Sleep of Reason* 109
  influenced by Brady and Hindley trial 109
Social Workers, employment of depends on recognition of various 'disorders' 22
'Softness', alleged characteristic of cannabis 80
Soma, fictional happiness drug invented by Aldous Huxley 83
  2,000 scientists involved in its (fictional) development 87
  arrival of Soma society distant prospect in 1970 95
  could not really exist 87
  used to quell riot 87
SOMA (Soma Research Association founded 1967) 96
  seeks to influence Wootton Report and separate cannabis from LSD 116

Spear, Henry Bryan (known as 'Bing') Home Office drugs adviser and friend to heroin addicts' 62
Spooning, unknown in Soviet Parks of Culture and Rest 90
SSRI (Selective Serotonin Re-Uptake Inhibitors) supposed 'antidepressant' drugs subject to increasing controversy about efficacy and side effects 15
  claim to treat 'depression' increasingly disputed 21
  prevalence of displaces old-fashioned psychiatry and neurology 20
Stevas, Norman St John (Lord St John of Fawsley) has ill-tempered brush with Callaghan 137
Storr, Anthony, signs advertisement in *The Times* 97
Strathclyde, Lord, confesses to past cannabis use 171
Straw, Jack, formally rejects Runciman report 192
Stroup, Keith, leading American campaigner for liberalizing drug laws 226
  claims to have been misrepresented 227–8
  interview with *Emory Wheel* 226–7
Sun, The slavish supporter of government of day, or party in ascendant, whatever it may be 168
Sunday Mirror
  publishes influential leak of Cabinet split on drugs 61

story perfectly true despite
 Crossman saying it wasn't 71
Sweden, policy on drugs favourably
 compared to that of Britain
 62, 264
  praised by Angela Watkinson
  MP 266
Swedish Army, study of conscripts
 suggests link between
 cannabis and mental illness 26
stupor, unfettered indulgence in
 considered as a right 3

'Talk to Frank', jokey and amoral
 site aimed at teenagers by
 government 249–50
Tannhauser (Wagner Opera) exalts
 virtues of oblivion 110
Taylor, Edward (MP) casts doubt
 on government grounds for
 restricting cigarette promotion
 36
temperance movement, valued
 self-discipline 54
  dead by 1970 88
  provides background for many
  Labour nonconformists 73
tetrahydracannabinol, principal
 active ingredient of cannabis
 27
  little known about its operation
  in 1967 115
Thatcher, Baroness Margaret
 blamed for delayed social
 consequences of 1960s
 revolution 121
  her economic liberalism
  closely allied with economic
  liberalism 251
  her supposedly conservative
  government continues
  moves towards cannabis
  decriminalisation 163–4
  her worshippers and her
  detractors fail to recognize
  liberal nature of her social
  policies 252
The Times
 advertisement blatant and crude
 142
 advertisement in, signatures on
 96–7
 advertisement summarized 142–3
 notorious advertisement in 72
 reputation and influence far
 greater than now 96
Third World, decriminalisation of
 drugs will help Britain down
 staircase to 11
Thomas, George, votes against
 liberalisation at decisive
 Cabinet meeting 73
thought, smothered by drug taking 3
tobacco, state has successfully used
 law to curb use of 30
Tobacco Manufacturers' Standing
 Committee, uses arguments
 similar to those now employed
 by cannabis lobby 32
trafficking, penalties for this
 mysteriously increased, as
 penalties for possession
 reduced 74
transubstantiation, Holy mystery
 easier to understand than
 mystery of evil nature of drugs
 66
'Treatment', name given to scheme
 for forcing taxpayers to
 supply Methadone and other
 substitutes to criminal abusers
 of illegal drugs 17–18

£900 million estimated annual
  cost 248
ineffectiveness of methadone
  248
large role of Methadone
  programme 248
treaty obligations, importance of in
  decriminalisation debate 79
triangulation, political deception
  technique 79

UFO Club, centre of 1960s
  counterculture 112
Untouchables, The (Film and TV
  series) from which most
  people get their ideas about
  US alcohol prohibition,
  causing them to think they
  know more than they do 55

Venusberg, symbol of profane love
  110
viagra, would have disturbed morals
  of 30 years ago 16
Vietnam War, 1960s generation
  marches righteously against xi

Walden, Brian (MP), signs
  advertisement in *The Times* 97
'War on Drugs', phantasmal xii
  hysteria gives impression that
  'War' is taking place 14
  non-existent 14
Watkinson, Angela (Conservative
  MP), her determination to
  resist consensus on Home
  Affairs Committee 264
  'minority report' 266
Wayne, Sir Edward
  his view accepted by Lord
  Hailsham 145
  wants small-scale cannabis
  possessors to escape prison
  145
Webb, Beatrice and Sidney
  mocked by Crosland for
  puritanism 90
  send honeymoon investigating
  trade societies 90
West Wittering, staidly respectable
  seaside village, scene of raid
  on Keith Richard and Mick
  Jagger 101
Widdecombe, Ann (politician) last
  major figure to seek to deter
  drug abuse with punishment
  167
  fellow Tories gleeful at her failure
  172
  her plan dropped from manifesto
  172
  made to look outmoded fool 172
  Shadow cabinet behaviour to 252
Whitehouse, Mary, briefly led
  conservative social movement
  121
Willetts, David, confesses past
  cannabis use 171
Wilson, Harold (Lord Wilson of
  Rievaulx) votes both ways on
  drugs in Cabinet split 65
  could have stayed in office till
  March 1971 75
Windlesham, Lord, Tory Minister
  who piloted Misuse of Drugs
  Bill through Lords, more
  relaxed on moral issues than
  Callaghan 82
Winehouse, Amy, singer, not charged
  after footage shown of her
  with substance that appeared
  to be crack cocaine 240

Wire, The (TV series) suggests that evils of drugs would end with legalisation 14
Wolf, Martin, seizes wrong end of stick with both hands 193
Woolton pie 94
Wootton, Barbara (Baroness Wootton of Abinger)
  appointed by Roy Jenkins 115
  bereaved by First World War 133
  British public under the impression she had been defeated 187
  her committee in being 114
  her prediction justified by events 268
  left-wing battle-axe 27
  mocks Ronald Butt's misunderstanding of true direction of drug policy 162
  not expected to produce conservative report 142
  not worried if child of her own smoked cannabis 134
  had no children 134
  pet donkeys 133
  prison 127
  quoted on ideals becoming commonplace 1
  religious unbeliever 133
  said cannabis less dangerous than alcohol 134
  self publicist 133
  thought polygamy 'perfectly possible' 133
  unmistakably a reformer 114
  whirlwind of radicalism in dumpy body 133
  worried about numbers of cannabis users sent to
Wootton Committee 27
  complacency of 150
  contrasted with Woolton Pie 94
  deliberations heavily influenced by cannabis lobby 72
  original title of 132
  report completed 71
  report reluctantly published 71
  SOMA seeks to influence 116
  still in session 141
  weakening of law their intention 71
Wootton Report
  acquits cannabis of charges not made against it 155
  battle over publication of report described 158–60
  Callaghan seeks to forestall 134
  contains many echoes of *Times* advertisement 145
  discusses slow growth of cannabis use 126
  racialist division of statistics 126
  reluctantly published by Callaghan 72
Wykehamists, emaciated but thoughtful 94

Young, Toby, candid admissions of 194–5